HIGH TICKET COURSES

The Fastest Way for Coaches, Consultants, and Service Providers to Make Six or Seven Figures with a New Hybrid Education Model

JOEL ERWAY

HIGH TICKET COURSES
The Fastest Way for Coaches, Consultants, and Service Providers to Make Six or Seven Figures with a New Hybrid Education Model

For permissions requests, bulk order purchases, and to inquire about prospective speaking engagements, podcast appearances, and mastermind talks, email maryjo@ thewebinaragency.com.

Betterway Enterprises Inc.
P.O. Box 361, Lewiston, NY 14092
highticketcourses.com
joelerway.com
thewebinaragency.com

ISBN: 978-1-7373107-0-9

Earnings Disclaimer: Every effort has been made to accurately represent our products and their potential to help our customers, their businesses, and/or their clients.

There is zero guarantee that you, or anyone following this material, will earn any money using the ideas in our materials, books, programs, or mentorship. Examples in these materials are not to be interpreted as a promise or guarantee of earnings. Earning potential is entirely dependent on the person using our product, ideas, and techniques. We do not position any products or services as a "get rich scheme."

Any claims made of actual earnings or examples of actual results can be verified upon request. Your level of success in attaining the results claimed in our materials depends on the time you devote to the ideas and techniques mentioned, your finances, knowledge, and various skills. Since these factors differ by individual, we cannot and do not guarantee your success or revenue generation, nor are we responsible for any of your actions related or not related to these materials.

Any and all forward-looking statements here or on any of our sales material are intended to express our opinion of earnings potential. Many factors will be important in determining your actual results and no guarantees are made that you will achieve results similar to ours or anybody else's. No guarantees are made that you will achieve any results from our ideas and techniques in these materials.

CONTENTS

DEDICATION

This book is dedicated to the world-changing digital experts who are making a massive impact while living a semi-retired lifestyle.

This book is for you.

We are semi-retired coaches, consultants,
and course creators.
We are the best in the world at what we do.
We choose with whom we work.
We get to decide how much money we make.
The money is only a byproduct of the value we create
in the world.

We change lives.
We make an impact.
We fight against outdated business methods.
We use modern methods that work.

We know that endlessly educating our market is a
waste of time.
People don't need more education.
They need more inspiration.
And while education can and sometimes
does lead to action,

people are far more motivated to
change and get results
when they have some skin in the game.

We do this by making them pay us a fair
price to solve their problems.
The industry teaches us to market, market,
market … then sell.
We throw that out the window.
For us, it's always sales over marketing.

The first thing a High Ticket Course Expert wants his
or her market to see is an *offer*.
Only after a prospect has shown interest in our offer
do we market to them further.
As High Ticket Course Experts, we are aware that
business growth for its own sake …
is a false god.

All the money in the world is worthless without the
time or energy to spend it.
Because of this, we optimize for happiness.
We take the time to enjoy our lives with our loved ones.
Our businesses are designed around our lives,
not the other way around.

High Ticket Course Experts achieve personal mastery
and professional excellence.
We live our lives in complete balance.
Because of this,
we're able to show up and serve others,
to lead them,
so they can become the best version of themselves.

FOREWORD

During the past 15 years as an entrepreneur, I've had an incredible amount of success when it comes to selling products online. In fact, I've sold more than $60 million worth of e-books and courses in three different industries.

But recently, selling products online has changed. Competition and advertising costs have increased dramatically. As a result, you need to spend years building out an entire library of courses in order to use paid ads and still make a profit. Personally, I started an online business so I could have more freedom in life—which meant I needed another solution.

I realized that offering a premium product at a premium price was the solution I was looking for, but I'd never sold a product for more than $1,500.

That's when I started studying Joel Erway's work and joined his High Ticket Courses program.

Joel has perfected the High Ticket Courses business model. I could have studied or called anyone in the world to learn how to implement this kind of business, but I invested in Joel because he knows exactly what he's doing. Most important of all: Everything he does and teaches is based on integrity and with the ultimate satisfaction of the customer in mind.

With Joel's guidance, we're now in the process of creating our first high ticket program, which is going to allow us to increase our profitability while also keeping our business as simple as possible.

Everything you're going to learn from Joel in this book—everything he teaches—is true. It works, and it will change your life if you use it.

—Mike Dillard,
Founder of Mike Dillard Media and
Host of the *Mike Dillard Podcast*

ADVANCE PRAISE

If business growth and marketing are what you're looking for, then I don't think you could invest in anything more valuable than reading and understanding the ideas and principles that Joel presents in this book. I can't say enough about Joel, his book, and his methodology. It's really some of **the most outstanding work I've seen in over 30 years of being on the front lines** of marketing. This book is likely going to become one of the most powerful marketing and sales books for 7-figure business owners in the next 12 to 24 months.

—**Russell Lundstrom,** Creator, Marketing Plan Formula

This is one of three books that will be on my desk at all times. Joel's methodology just makes so much sense. It keeps us away from shiny object syndrome, which, as entrepreneurs, we all suffer from. He makes it super, super simple. Read the book. Follow the steps. You will see results. If you don't get anything else from this book, get these four magic words: *Make The Damn Offer*. Because that is the thing so many of us miss. I cannot wait to share this with pretty much everybody that I know.

—**Ely Delaney,** Automated Systems Strategist Creator, Follow Up Rockstar System

Joel is an absolute monster when it comes to **taking an idea and turning that idea into a six- or seven-figure business**, and his entire methodology is condensed into this book. If I could go back and start my journey again, the first thing I would do is buy this book. I would study it every single day. Then, I would basically take all my money and throw it to Joel because I honestly think he has the capacity to change your life more than anyone else I've ever met.

—**Jason Watson,** Direct Response Copywriter,
Owner of Spectrum Media Agency

I wish I had had this book years ago when I first started in this online world. The information Joel shares with you in this book is gold. It will shed so much light on **how to be profitable in the online world—a lot faster than you would otherwise.** I had spent at least two years trying to get clients … Within one week of implementing Joel's program, I had at least 20 highly-qualified leads that had actually applied to speak with me on the phone.

He explains why you would want to start with a high ticket course versus a tiny offer. Then he goes into great detail on how you would attract your ideal client, straight from how to acquire them, how to get them to apply, and then how to enroll them. It takes you through the whole customer journey process and how to structure your high ticket course. I can't believe he went into such great detail. Pick it up. Read it. I highly recommend it. It'll make a huge difference.

—**Dr. Emily Stopper,** Founder & CEO, The Happy Dentist

This book is not based on internet fads or trickery or shiny objects. It's based on humans and how humans act. If you have specialized knowledge and you want to help other people with that specialized knowledge, do what this book says: **Take the fundamentals, put them into a minimum viable funnel, and then make the offer.** This book isn't just about how to make a funnel or how to do sales. It's also about how to do the back-end, how to do delivery, how to make an offer that matches what you want to do. It's about how you want to live your lifestyle.

—**Rick Friesen,** CEO, Contractor Convergence

My heart was racing as I read this book. This book lays out the entire framework for how to create an incredibly success-ful business. **If you're a coach, a consultant, a salesperson, a marketer, or a course creator, this book is your Bible.** We've been taught that we need to indoctrinate and engage our audi-ence first and provide all this incredible value and content for them before they start to know, like, and trust us. Joel has proven that you don't have to do that at all. Read this book, and you will save yourself months and years of banging your head against the wall. People who want your high ticket service are looking for you. And Joel teaches you how to deliver your messaging, how to frame it, and how to sell it without selling. He lays it all out for you from A to Z. He gives you the scripts, tells you exactly what to do, and he gives you the entire frame-work to do it.

—**Dean Edelson**, Owner, 1 Big Idea Marketing

If you're an entrepreneur who is struggling to build a coaching and consulting business, you definitely want to read this book. Joel Erway is brilliant. He is, hands down, my #1 go-to coach because not only does he have a heart for helping you and giving you real strategies to grow your business, but **it's all in this book**.

—**Karwanna Dyson,** Government Contracts Strategist,
She's Got Goals, LLC

I was hooked just after reading the dedication section, as I found it to be a brilliant marketing piece in itself. There were so many golden nuggets just in the first section. I've been in sales and marketing for over 15 years now, so I've seen and been through my fair share of different methodologies, strategies, and frameworks. However, it wasn't until I stumbled upon Joel and his descension model that things really started to click. The biggest impact this book had for me was what Joel calls "closest to the conversion hole" methodology. **If you just apply this *one thing* in your business, you could totally transform your results.**

—**Sonny Wong,** Creator, Diamond Mind Activation

Before reading Joel's book, I was having all these thoughts and ideas around what I could do and what I couldn't do and what I didn't know. They were holding me back from taking action. After reading Joel's book, though, I realized it was really easy. I was able to implement things right away.

It's not only very step-by-step and very practical but also very inspiring. **I walked away saying to myself, *I can do this*. And I did.** I now have kick-ass positioning and an amazing offer. I have a webinar, and I'm doing Facebook ads. These are things that I never thought I would be able to do. And the best part? I enjoyed the process because Joel makes the process enjoyable. Get Joel's book. Then take action.

—**Cristina DiGiacomo**, Founder, MorAlchemy

"Joel is FIRE … I've spent over four days with Joel in person. He *gets it.*"

—**Scott Oldford**, Founder, ScottOldford.com

When I met Joel, I was struggling to reach my ideal client. I had a great coaching service, but I just didn't have my messaging down. I didn't have all the pieces in the right order. **Very quickly, Joel helped me get from cold traffic to booked sales consultations to high ticket clients.**

Now, my coaching practice is thriving, and it's really all due to Joel's efforts to help me finally understand what I had to do to get my messaging right. Starting with the Power Offer and using his mini webinar methodology. Read this book cover to cover. Absorb what Joel says. His unique ideas around sales and marketing will help you get high ticket clients so you, too, can achieve the semi-retired lifestyle.

—**Brad Wachter**, Founder, GrayHairTrader.com

Take a chance on yourself because you're not taking a chance on Joel. The system's proven, and it's worth it.

—**Zan Shaikh,** Founder, Rankone and Bright Vision Digital

Before reading this book, it took me over a year to help my clients reach six-figures because I was following the Ascension Model, which is very popular advice. It requires a lot of effort, and a lot of trial and error, and you are never 100 percent sure whether it will work out or not.

My AHA moment came when Joel described the Descension Model. Since I started applying what Joel talks about in this book, **I have now been able to help my clients reach six-figures in only two months.**

Joel also talks about building your business for scale and not for burnout. That totally resonated with me. With this particular model and approach, there's a lot more excitement to do the work, it's a lot more fun, and most importantly, it's simple.

—**Sanjay Yadav,** Creator, Attract Your Audience

Before working with Joel, all of my past clients were organic and referrals … Joel wrote an absolutely stellar ad for us which quickly began to resonate with cold traffic. And it immediately resulted in at least one sales call per day for my high ticket coaching offer.

—**Brett Stewart,** Founder, Inner Edge

Going through this book sequentially was helpful to me because I was able to see exactly what I needed to do to get to a place of peace in my business instead of constant chaos. **What I love about this book is its simplicity.** For me, it brought a lot of clarity. It's very clear and simple to go through and follow. Thanks to Joel and the High Ticket Courses community, I'm able to accomplish more and do less, so that I have time to experience a semi-retired lifestyle with my family.

—**Audie Cashion,** Dental ONE Thing Coach & Speaker, Audie Cashion International, LLC

One of the best parts of this program was the INSTANT ROI. Before I received any training, I was able to implement just one piece of advice that gave me an instant $11K. That was before I had my mini-webinar up! Just goes to show that Joel is a marketing genius, and everyone should be doing this.

—Neal Samudre

This book is spot-on. Prior to learning from Joel, I made the mistake of actually creating a full-blown course before I tested it, wasting months and months of my time and discovering I had the wrong audience. By joining one of Joel's programs, I learned that **the offer needs to be tested, and then you build the course as you go**. Doing so allowed us to test the offer first and then scale afterward.

The other thing that I learned from Joel was to have a very streamlined course. I learned to streamline my messaging to make sure that it is digestible, and I learned about being hands-on with my students. With Joel's knowledge and expertise, I was able to get from point A to point B a lot faster. Joel is a great mentor for the high ticket space, and I highly recommend not only Joel but also his book.

Don't hesitate. Grab the book. Read it. Do what it says.

—Ian Bentley, CEO & Founder, PivotandScale.com

When I saw Joel, it's like he held out this long branch and said, "Grab on, I'm going to pull you out right now," and just pulled me to freedom.

—Darren Chabluk, Founder, DrDone

Susan Lassiter-Lyons shared a link.
April 16 at 9:20 PM · 🌐

Welp, this new business I launched Sept 9th has done $187,900 in sales so far. $165,666 collected. List of 3,500. 50 absolute dream clients. Multiple 5-star reviews on Google My Business. Ad spend of $34,978. All from my poolside home office and mainly in my underpants.

Thanks so much for the support and guidance Joel, Jeremy, and Brendan. Couldn't have done it without you guys.

I did everything Joel Erway taught us—literally, verbatim, and step-by-step. I tossed aside my ego and took advantage of every opportunity for support and feedback. And in the last 6 weeks as a result of this program, I've made 28 sales calls, 11 sales. $37,800 collected, and 7.4X [return] on my ad spend. I read a letter I wrote to myself on June 4th when I was hopeless and lost, and I don't even recognize that person anymore. Thank you doesn't even begin to cover it. You guys gave me back my confidence and gave me hope. And I am deeply, forever grateful.

—**Susan Lassiter-Lyons**, CEO, Lassiter Publishing Group

The Origin of High Ticket Courses

Where the Method Began

Staring at the ceiling fan, overcome with anxiety, I was ready to lose another night's sleep. This had become a pretty typical situation for me over the past few months.

It was 2016, and we had just moved into our dream home, which was three times more expensive than our previous home. My wife gave birth to our first child, Dominic. She was no longer working, so I was the sole provider (with another mouth to feed), and our living expenses had tripled.

My stress and anxiety were at an all-time high. Every night, I was lying awake in bed wondering to myself: *Where's my next client coming from? Where am I going to get my next customer?*

I had just spent the past year and a half hiring mentors, joining masterminds, and paying tens of thousands of dollars to solve this problem, but I felt like I was no closer to the solution. I was completely frustrated with myself. It seemed as though everything that I had been trying wasn't working. I was following all the gurus, all the typical advice, but there I was at 11 p.m., unable to sleep. Again.

Whenever this happened, I went into consumption mode. I read, I studied, I tried to find good ideas. I studied those who were successful. And while I had paid a lot of money to masterminds and expensive coaches, I was still stuck.

As I was lying in bed that night, fear consumed me. Fear that I wasn't going to be able to make it—that I wasn't cut out for this. Fear that I was going to have to go back and get a day job.

I worried about what my wife was going to think about me. I worried about what others would say. I worried that I'd have to put my tail between my legs and go back to living a more traditional life—a life that I knew but didn't want. I had lived the life of an entrepreneur for two years, and I had come too far to go back.

That night, I picked up a book by Bob Bly called *How to Create Irresistible Offers*[1].

At the beginning of the book, there's a chart that talks about the cost to acquire a customer related to the type of content you put out (we'll go into detail in Chapter 8). Essentially, what it was saying is: If your content is more offer-driven, then the cost to acquire a customer is going to be the lowest. If your content is more brand-driven, it will cost you more to acquire that customer.

Now, this was only within the first few pages of the book, but as soon as I read that, it was like the parting of the Red Sea. I've read so many great books, but this was the moment that changed my path and turned the ship in the right direction in what might be described as a quantum leap.

---

[1] Robert W. Bly, *How to Create Irresistible Offers: The Easiest Way on Earth to Make Your Marketing Generate More Leads, Orders, and Sales* (Delray Beach, FL: American Writers & Artists, 2009), p. 3.

	PERFORMANCE DEGRADATION AS BRAND CONTENT INCREASES AND OFFER CONTENT DECREASES		
Copy Platform	**Brand Content**	**Offer Content**	**Approximate Cost Per Sale**
Primarily Offer-Driven	10%	90%	$50-$100
Offer Leads – Brand Follows	25%	75%	$200-$250
Brand Leads – Offer Follows	75%	25%	$400-$600
Primarily Brand-Driven	90%	10%	$800-$1,000

Everything that I had been doing up until that point was what all the typical marketers tell you to do. You put out content, put out content, put out content, educate, educate, educate, and then eventually somebody is going to want to buy. But this chart in Bob Bly's book said the exact opposite. It said that if you want people to buy, you need to make more offers.

My interpretation of the chart:

Make the Damn Offer!

What I had been trying over the past two years in order to acquire customers was education-based marketing. But this approach is expensive, unpredictable, unreliable, and unsustainable for most people with an unproven offer.

And at that moment—when I saw that chart—I realized what my problem was: My cost-per-customer acquisition was high because I was over-educating my market and not giving them an opportunity to buy.

I knew that if I were able to solve this problem, I would never have to worry about feeding my family. I would never have to worry about being perceived as a failure. And I would never have to worry about going out and finding a job.

So that night, I ran downstairs. I thought: *I've got it. Everything I've been doing has been backward, and tonight I'm going to flip it on its head. I'm going to solve this.*

By 11:57 p.m., I hit publish on my computer and posted my first Power Offer, and went to bed. The next day, I had closed one $25K client, and I had a second $25K client on the waitlist. Literally overnight, I produced two $25K clients!

This was the birth of the High Ticket Courses (HTC) model.

Don't Trust It Until You Test It

"Hey, Alex," I said, "I tried something new the other day on my own business, and I would love for us to test it out with you. I think it's going to crush it. Are you open to testing?"

Alex said, "Sure, man, I'm open to doing whatever, as long as it gets results."

Alex had been struggling to get his business off the ground. He came to me with some big ideas but zero revenue from his coaching program. His primary source of income came from flying all over the country, helping gym owners launch and grow their memberships.

Within 24 hours, we had his system up and running. We immediately started generating leads and appointments for Alex at around $10 each. By the end of the first day, Alex's calendar was absolutely full.

Alex was able to take those appointments and start closing deals for $5K to $10K each.

I remember Alex messaging me over the next couple of days. Every time he got a new appointment, he would text me: "Just got another one!" He was texting me three, four, or five times a day.

Alex used the system we developed to help launch his business and go from zero to $400K per month *in the first six months*. He's gone on to grow his company to epic proportions. Last I heard, he's done over $90 million online. In light of full transparency, growing any business to $90 million requires much more than a compelling offer. But we were happy to provide the launchpad and kickstart for the momentum.

Alex   Joel Erway took us from literally $0/mo with a concept to $400k/mo in 6 months. His deep level of understanding is insane in this one type of pitch that he has specialized in. Totally worth the money (obviously). Buy whatever he sells you because he is such a moral guy he will keep delivering until you feel bad he is still making you more money.

After testing out my new customer acquisition method on my own business and validating my methods with Alex, I knew that it wasn't just a fluke for me.

At this point, though, all I really had was an idea and a couple of case studies. I didn't have any course content or training materials put together. All I had were my results and my confidence that I could get those results for other people.

I decided to formalize this system and test it with some other clients.

I started working with a few clients on a one-on-one basis. Obviously, working one-on-one with someone requires a higher investment than if they were to go through my DIY training. So, I sold the highest ticket *first* and got those results without even building out my course. I focused on getting feedback from my clients. I documented the exact methods they needed and wanted to learn. And as I made money, I built my course.

I knew that this was the start of something really big. Very quickly, I grew a waiting list of clients.

There was something powerful about the system I was developing. I finally had cash flow coming in the door, so I could reinvest into my system and scale down my product line in a way that didn't eat up all my time and financial resources. This paradigm shift began my journey of generating millions of dollars through the HTC model.

I dissected and developed my system. I threw away everything that wasn't putting money in my bank account, and I stumbled on a business model that was the exact opposite of what I had been taught.

No More "Feast or Famine"

In this book, I'm going to teach you how to develop a business model around your expertise. I'm going to show you how to structure your offers so you don't get stuck in a feast or famine situation, scrambling to find clients to keep your business afloat. I'm also going to show you one of the most valuable assets that you can create in your business: the customer who will buy from you again and again.

Most experts aren't taught how to actually design their offers and business model. As a result, they're left feeling lost and confused.

Many will end up giving away the farm and cannibalizing their offers. On the flip side, many will end up selling their expertise on a dollars-per-hour basis, stuck in the one-to-one coaching model with no clear path for scale. This is easily avoidable *if* you understand the right way to structure your offers and position yourself in the marketplace.

There's a time and place for both productization and one-on-one offers, but many experts aren't able to extract themselves out of either model. You have to have a clear path to get yourself out of a one-on-one model and scale your business without cannibalizing your offers.

It all comes down to having the right business model for your High Ticket Offer.

A Cautionary Tale of Three Experts

As an expert, there's a right way and a wrong way to enroll more clients into your programs and services.

The wrong way severely limits your potential for growth, whereas the right way will give you complete and total freedom in ways you never thought possible.

Let's take a deeper dive with three examples:

Meet Bob

Bob is a consultant who helps companies increase their revenue through different proprietary methods and operational efficiencies.

Bob has a laundry list of clients that he's worked with over the last 20+ years in business. He is well-respected in his industry and is well-positioned as an authority.

But Bob has one big problem: He spends way too much time marketing his business to get clients, and he's burned out.

Bob has implemented many different sales and marketing tactics that might spike his revenue over some months, but he sees that revenue dip back just as fast as it grew.

He lacks stability. And he goes through cycles of anxiety and fear as he experiences dry spells without clients.

Bob suffers from "The Hustler's Conundrum." He realizes that he needs to "hustle" to get more clients.

That hustle looks like this:

>Ask his friends if he can be on their podcast ...

>Try to land more speaking gigs ...

>Email his subscribers ...

>Launch more episodes of his own podcast ...

>Guest blogging …

>Post on social media five times per day about his "new offer" ...

>Cold LinkedIn outreach to 100 new leads per day ...

Anything to get more clients.

Meet Ben

Ben is a passionate, intelligent, and very motivated individual with a skill set he wishes to teach others. He decides to start this as a side hustle that will hopefully turn into a viable business one day.

He sees all sorts of "courses" for sale ranging from $5, $100, and $1,000+.

Being a newbie with no prior marketing experience, he starts searching and following influencers to see what they are doing.

Eventually, he decides that because he has no established following, he must first build an audience so he can build trust and a relationship with them.

He decides to create lots of free and low-cost content to attract and build that audience with the hopes that someday they will trust him enough to buy more expensive courses from him.

Ben struggles to get any traction with this model.

His audience that he curated from his free content rarely purchases anything from him. After months of struggling, he's barely made a couple hundred dollars—not even enough to cover his software expenses.

Even worse, he feels that producing more content for his freebie-seeking audience is becoming an obligation. And one that has turned his passion into dread ...

Now, Meet Beth

Beth has developed her programs and offers the right way, which gives her the two most valuable freedom currencies: **time and money.**

Beth is a self-proclaimed "semi-retiree," choosing to work with her clients about three to four hours per day.

Beth helps women develop an "Infinite Income" strategy that allows them to retire early. When she's not working with them, she's playing tennis or lounging by the pool at her country club in Palm Springs.

Beth is able to attract new customers and clients at will because she has dialed in the perfect offer that generates a response from people who've never heard of her. She's confident that her course is the perfect fit for her clients, having built it according to their needs and desires, and scaled it in a way that didn't overburden her.

She has more money without the severe revenue dips because even in her slowest months, she has built a trusted audience of people who want her offer. She has the ability to choose how big or how small she wants her business to be because she has built her own "demand faucet," which gives her the ability to turn the client flow on or off easily.

Who would you rather be? Bob, Ben, or Beth?

Unfortunately, there are way more Bobs and Bens than there are Beths. But if you choose to follow Beth's path—the High Ticket Courses path—you will reap tremendous benefits.

You'll have the freedom to spend more time traveling with your family or pursuing your passions because it's not spent chasing down prospects or endlessly promoting yourself.

And you'll serve your clients in a more leveraged way that's more beneficial for both you and them.

Want to join Beth?

Read on.

Numbers Don't Lie

Let's assume you're selling a course for $200, and you're looking to get to $30K a month, which is $1,000 a day, right?

That means you need 150 sales per month!

And let's say that the sales system you've chosen to use is fairly typical, and you're getting a 1% to 2% conversion rate. Let's be generous and call it 2%. (Sadly, the most typical conversion rate for people just starting their business is actually zero ... but we can't use that.)

So, 150 people at a 2% conversion rate means you need to find 7,500 qualified people every month. And it's these kinds of numbers that make most people think that they need to build a massive email list or a large audience on social media before making any money. Crazy, huh?

Now, just imagine you're selling your course for $5,000.

At $5,000, instead of needing 150 sales, you only need six.

An interesting thing happens when you only need a few sales: You're able to laser-target ideal buyers and experience much higher conversion rates. I'll show you how in a bit. For now, let's take the same 2% conversion rate, to be conservative.

Well, then you only need to get your offer in front of 300 people!

And remember, that's to get to $30K/month.

You could get one sale and make $5,000 just by getting your offer in front of 50 qualified people.

Now, doesn't that sound achievable?

The right sales model—combining your assets in the right way, at the right time, and marketing to the right people—can virtually make or break your business!

Who Is the Ideal High Ticket Course Expert?

The ideal High Ticket Course Expert looks like this:

- Coaches who love serving their clients and helping them get transformational results, but struggle to consistently attract new clients into their business.

- Coaches and service providers who work one-on-one with clients, want to stop trading time for money, and are looking for a more leveraged way to grow their business.

- Everyday course creators who've struggled to make $10,000+/month consistently and want to include a high-end, premium version of their course.

The Choice Is Yours

As an expert who has the knowledge, skillset, and ability to help people, you get to design the life you want. It's totally up to you what you'll do with the time you'll save and the newly found revenue you'll enjoy by following the High Ticket Courses method outlined in this book.

Keep in mind that experts who choose the HTC model aren't looking for completely passive revenue. They choose to work—when they want, with whomever they want, on any project they want.

Why?

Because they *want* to.

They want meaningful work balanced with meaningful relationships. And they have a set of core values and beliefs:

- They pursue more than just a single sale.
- They leverage their intellectual property into different versions of their core promise in the form of programs that meet the needs of their audience.
- They value the ability to choose what they want, when they want it, and how they want to get it.
- They prioritize speed and execution to get results.
- They are up front with their intentions so their prospects and customers trust them. Developing a good relationship with their audience is vital to their business.
- They buy paid ads to Leverage their time—so it's not spent "hustling"—to get their message out faster and to more people.
- They only focus on needle-moving activities that support their growth.
- They value freedom above all else.

They pursue the semi-retired life.

Who Is Joel Erway?

If you don't love your work, you won't love your clients. And that won't make it easy to love your life.

Believe me, I know what I'm talking about.

I've spent six years trying to crack the code so that I could live a semi-retired life while building a multiple-7-figure business. The road to get here was not easy, but I am living proof that it is possible.

If you're a consultant, coach, or service provider, then I already know you're sick and tired of marketing that you have little control over. You've tried it all: networking at your local events (ahem … begging for business), word of mouth, social media marketing, LinkedIn, cold outreach, and referrals. These marketing methods are straight-up unreliable and unpredictable, leaving you feeling on top of the world one day and at rock bottom the next.

You've worked hard to get where you are, and you deserve a reliable method you can count on. Most importantly, you need a business model that can help you get to that next level.

Enter: High Ticket Courses.

There is a way to attract your perfect-fit customers without developing an endless machine. A realistic, sustainable technique to predictably increase your monthly revenue by 5-figures every month in a leveraged way that allows you to live free.

You've already found your specialty, now you want to get to that $30K to $50K per month without having to sift through leads for your ideal customer. The way to achieve this is not pumping out massive amounts of content, selling a low-ticket offer, or creating freebie lead magnets.

I have developed a new business model that has worked time and time again for helping High Ticket Course Experts launch and scale their courses while designing a lifestyle around what is most important to them. In fact, it's so powerful that it's helped some of my clients scale to the tune of $20K, $50K, and $400K per month and beyond—without the need for the "Ascension Model."

And I'm here to share it with you.

I didn't just wake up one day and have it all figured out. I've spent time, money, and sleepless nights trying to figure out the "golden solution" to making webinars that would convert.

After six years of giving sales presentations and spending money on masterminds, I became an agency owner, helping other people launch and sell their courses. In 2015, I decided to try to launch my own courses to scale my business by educating, using all the funnel techniques I had learned. I quickly realized these tactics were not working.

Here I was—founder of "The Webinar Agency"—and my own webinars were not converting. Not a good look.

I finally asked myself, "What if the way I've been learning isn't the end-all-be-all way to succeed?"

So I decided to blaze my own trail. I built a 7-figure hybrid agency using a new model. No webinars, lead magnets, cold outreach, or hustling. And I want to take you along for the ride, so you don't waste your time and money like I did. You can spend more time living the life you want by designing a model that works for you. And you deserve that.

In my experience, the most valuable currency isn't money—it's *time*.

I've built a 4x4 (4 hours a day, 4 days per week) work week so I can dedicate more time to my family. Each morning I go for a 90-minute ruck (a military-inspired exercise that involves walking with a weighted vest or backpack) around town, and Fridays are reserved for making pancakes with my kids. I'm able to do all of this while running a 7-figure business. And there's no reason you can't do the same.

I'll show you a way to spend less time building everything you think you need to attract clients. They're already out there, wanting exactly what you're offering. The only problem is that you're targeting the wrong group.

Don't just cast a wide net and hope something sticks. In this book, we'll go over how to stop playing the numbers game and how to start validating your offer. We will focus on activating an optimal customer acquisition process that will consistently work for you— rather than against you.

When you can significantly cut down the time you spend finding your ideal prospects, you essentially give yourself the gift of time. And what you do with that time is completely up to you. Want to spend more time with your family? Work on a passion project? Get out in nature more? You're the boss. You can choose what to do with your time currency.

My goal for you is to be able to develop the perfect model and offer, for the perfect audience, that allows you to develop the perfect lifestyle-business for you.

This will put you in the driver's seat.

All you have to do is follow the guide and watch it work its magic.

Semi-Retirement Personified

Years ago, I was shopping for a new truck. My sales associate and I were on the lot where he was showing me a wide variety of trucks and explaining all the features and benefits. We were looking at black trucks and crew cabs and double cabs, and diesel trucks versus gasoline trucks.

As we were looking at a beautiful, black 2019 Chevy Silverado Custom Crew Cab, another customer pulled up beside us and asked my sales rep, "Hey, have you seen Mike?"

My sales rep said, "Oh, Mike? No, he's not in today. He's kind of *semi-retired*. He just comes and goes as he pleases and deals with a select few customers, on his own terms, on his own schedule."

That's it! I thought. *That's what I am! I'm semi-retired!* Up to then, I just didn't have a name for it.

I could never get on board with the full-retirement lifestyle. It sounded all well and good, lying on the beach and sipping cocktails.

But for crying out loud, I'm still young, so I have a ton of energy. And there's so much I want to pursue. I have things I want to accomplish … people I want to help … milestones I want to achieve.

Full-blown retirement doesn't serve most people, let alone somebody who's in the prime of their life.

Semi-retirement is the ideal life. It's being able to work when you want, on the projects that you want, however much you want, how often you want, with as much or little effort as you want.

If you want to work 40 hours a week, that's totally fine. I know plenty of entrepreneurs who work more than 40 hours a week because that's what they want. But if you want to work 10 to 20 hours a week, and make sure you've got Fridays off with your family and kids, or make sure you're able to take a couple of months off in the summer to do whatever you want, that's totally cool, too.

Building a business around your lifestyle, a business you love, a business that serves your life—*that's* semi-retirement.

There are some days when I put in more hours than usual. On average, though, I try to maintain a "four hours per day, four days per week," working model. I take Friday, Saturday, and Sunday off every single week. I have designed my life so I can live it to the fullest.

I'm all about living a semi-retired lifestyle. I always think, "What's the least amount of effort I need to put in to get the most amount of reward on the back end?" That's pretty much how I came to distill all possibilities down to "the shortcut."

When I discovered the High Ticket Courses model, it was a revolutionary shift in how I approached the online course and coaching industry. I used to think that I needed to focus on one or the other (meaning courses OR coaching) for simplicity. But that wasn't the case.

What I discovered was that there was a simple, effective way to build this model and bring it to market without complex marketing or sales funnels, and without confusing my audience.

Today, I help other experts shortcut their way to hyper-profitable online courses and coaching programs that can be grown and sustained.

Collectively, I've made tens of millions for myself and my clients through the methods you'll read here (unofficially, we've likely surpassed an estimated $100 million, but I can't verify the exact numbers). Don't worry though, you won't see me posing next to some flashy, red Corvette.

I'm a former engineer-turned-course-marketer from Upstate New York, born in the mid-80s, currently living in a little ol' village north of Niagara Falls. I gripe about the cold weather like I'm 82 and wonder why we don't live in Florida full time, but we retreat from the brutal winters of Niagara Falls to the sunny beaches of St. Augustine for about a month every year, living that #SemiRetired life.

My guilty pleasure is riding my Cub Cadet mower 'round my lawn every Thursday, and then I enjoy posting pictures about how awesome my lawn looks versus my neighbors' lawns. Yep, I'm just a bit of a nerd.

In 2015, I helped my first client boost their sales by 1,400% in just two weeks. Since then, I've launched a multi-7-figure business using my own High Ticket Courses model. I've also helped hundreds of students and clients successfully launch, grow, and scale their own digital courses and programs.

Ultimately, we build our businesses to allow us to live a semi-retired lifestyle—which looks different for everyone.

By the end of this book, you're going to understand the real opportunity in harnessing what you already know and packaging it in a way that pays you good money, predictably, day after day.

Once you develop your intellectual property and package it into different sellable assets, you will create your own client- and customer-generating machine without the hustle—and become a High Ticket Course Expert.

What Are the High Ticket Courses Goals?

There are several goals for a High Ticket Course. I want you to keep these goals in mind as you go through this book because as you start to run your own business model, you'll start to gather data, and you'll need to remember why you really set this up in the first place.

1. You want the ability to use an online learning platform to create a legitimate lifestyle for your business. I can't express enough how much this allows you to create leverage by demonstrating your expertise while teaching and sharing your knowledge.

2. You want a business model that will create multiple streams of income through the various levels of service with your overall program. (We're going to discuss this more later when we start to develop the different tiers of done-for-you, done-with-you, and do-it-yourself.)

3. You want to be positioned as an authority within your marketplace and hold a position of influence. You want a business model that is designed to help you establish your brand positioning.

4. The final—and most important—goal is to have the ability to rapidly scale with paid traffic and run your sales system with minimal effort.

Everything in this book is about leveraging your expertise into a simple, scalable business model.

The HTC model provides you with a simplistic plan and approach to design, launch, leverage, and scale your expert-based business with two to three versions of your core offer.

It allows you to package your intellectual property, knowledge, and skill sets in a way that is clearly valuable for your customers.

It gives you more consistency in your business by adding multiple streams of revenue.

And it gives you the ability to escape the "hustler's conundrum" by developing an offer and sales system that consistently attracts new buyers into your programs—without hustling nonstop.

The HTC model teaches you how to take advantage of your most valuable asset: your Intellectual Property (IP). Far too many people don't know how to stop giving away value for free and just Make the Damn Offer (MTDO). This book is about to change all that.

CHAPTER 1

DISCOVER THE HIGH TICKET COURSES (HTC) MODEL

If It's Good Enough for Tesla ...

Little does he know, Elon Musk helped me to experience a massive shift when I read a post on his Tesla blog back in 2016. He put a crack in the Ascension Model that I had been following to try to grow my business. He also changed my perspective and taught me about patience and persistence.

Here's what he wrote in his July 20, 2016, Tesla.com/blog/master-plan-part-deux post:

Master Plan, Part Deux

Elon Musk July 20, 2016

The first master plan that I wrote 10 years ago is now in the final stages of completion. It wasn't all that complicated and basically consisted of:

Create a low volume car, which would necessarily be expensive

Use that money to develop a medium volume car at a lower price

Use *that* money to create an affordable, high volume car

And...

Provide solar power. No kidding, this has literally been on our website for 10 years.

This was the confirmation I needed, after reading Bob Bly's *How to Create Irresistible Offers*, to completely flip my business model on its head. *Upside down.*

Nothing so simple had ever made such a big impact in my life than learning how Elon Musk launched his multibillion-dollar automobile brand. Because if the idea was good enough—and worked—for Elon Musk, it should be good enough—and work—for me.

There's a huge difference between following the Ascension Model, where you start with a freebie or low-ticket item and then try to upsell, upsell, upsell, versus Elon's model of starting high and then downselling, downselling, downselling—especially in digital marketing, when you don't have the time or money to wait for better days ahead.

Sure, Elon Musk had venture capitalists with tons of capital, but he still went this route because he knew he needed to eventually fund his own solar power startup.

Build for Scale, Not for Burnout

Just because you sell a course or have coaching clients, that doesn't mean you have a scalable business model.

As someone who's built and managed dozens of webinar funnels for course creators, I was naturally drawn to the Course Creator

Model: create a sales webinar, run Facebook ads, and sell lots of $300–$2K DIY low-ticket courses.

Are there marketers out there who are successful with this model? Yes. I've worked with many of them.

But the reality is that this is a pipe dream for more than 99% of course creators. Here's why: Building a sales webinar funnel is like the holy grail of marketing. You need to get a lot of things right to make it click. And frankly, most people don't have the where-withal to stick it through because it costs a lot of time and money with no guarantee it will work.

Also, selling DIY courses provides very little satisfaction or fulfill-ment. Yes, you'll help people. But you won't build the intimate relationship with the customers that provides the real enjoyment we get as experts sharing our knowledge.

Finally, running a sales webinar and selling courses is not a business model. It's a promotion. Promotions have a start and end date. They have a lifespan. One day it will work, then all of a sudden, your market will be sick of it, and it will lose its effectiveness.

Does this mean we shouldn't sell low ticket courses? Absolutely not. We just need to incorporate DIY courses in the right order. And if you're in the early stages of launching your course offer, the DIY version should not be the first thing you sell.

In the early days of running The Webinar Agency, I quickly real-ized that I did not want to scale that company and its done-for-you services through growing a large team.

Management was not my skill set, nor did I desire to learn it. I was perfectly happy with our little team of five or six employees and contractors. So, I decided to scale through a low ticket course.

At the time, what I thought I needed was completely separate marketing with a separate sales funnel to promote this course. So, I spent months building that course-specific funnel, only to realize it didn't work.

Hundreds of hours and tens of thousands of dollars were spent on that project, only to see it thrown in the trash.

Even worse, my attention had gone away from the agency, so client acquisition was lower than normal. That meant I needed to hustle to get more clients, or else we'd run out of cash. That's a recipe for burnout.

Thankfully, I discovered that I didn't need to create multiple funnels and sales methods to acquire coaching or course clients. I could attract them all through one simple, direct sales process which would make my client and customer acquisition process infinitely more effective. And, I could use this exact same sales process to test new offers without creating new marketing campaigns.

HTC Tiers and Trajectory

I want to give you a bird's-eye view of the High Ticket Courses business model. Then, I'll break it down in later chapters.

The High Ticket Courses model helps you to leverage your time and resources to grow beyond selling just one version of your program, service, or course. The model has two main parts: The Tiers and The Trajectory.

1. Understanding your core promise and *how* to create two to three versions of your core promise to fit a larger number of your audience (The Tiers).
2. Understanding *when* to implement those different versions and how to market them (The Trajectory).

I'm going to give you an overview of the HTC model and then take you through it step by step in later chapters. If you don't understand it all at first, that's ok. It will make more sense later on as we go.

In fact, I want to encourage you to read or listen to this book once for understanding and then go back a second time, implementing as you go.

Start at the Top Tier and Work Your Way Down

If you don't already have a course created, you will start at the top with Tier 3—the most personalized level—and scale down. This is called the Descension Model. As you do this, your audience gets bigger, and you're able to develop more leveraged programs. This way, you can educate and serve your current audience while building an audience that is looking to buy your coaching programs and courses.

- **Tier 3:** Your most premium and personalized version of your promise, which could be either one-on-one consulting or done-for-you. If you're an agency and you already have a done-for-you offer, you already have your Tier 3.

- **Tier 2:** These are your mid-ticket programs. Here you have coaching, done-with-you assistance, and many other versions of offers that are more leveraged (which nobody talks about in the coaching world).

- **Tier 1:** Your most productized version: Do-it-yourself (DIY) training, workshops, and low-ticket offers.

THE HIGH TICKET COURSES DESCENSION MODEL

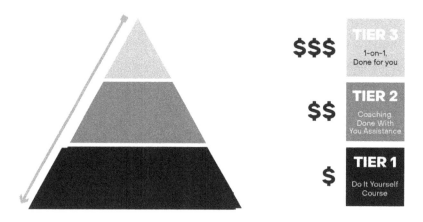

As you look at this model, you might think this looks a little "backward." That's because you're probably more familiar with the Ascension Model, which is what many people in the digital marketing community promote.

The Ascension Model starts by first giving something of value away for free to build an audience. Then, as you ascend that audience up your value ladder by offering them a low-ticket item, they will (theoretically) buy your higher ticket offer later.

Does the Ascension Model work? Yes, but only for brands and companies who can afford to build big lists and be out-of-pocket thousands of dollars in marketing and ads—for months at a time—testing campaigns. It's extremely risky for the experts and solopreneurs who are relying on cash on hand *now*. They can't afford to risk these types of campaigns.

Instead, we are going in the opposite direction to focus on one single sales process for making direct offers of our high end programs and services *first*. Then, we'll downsell to those who aren't ready or able to afford our top tier. This is the most effective and economical approach to building your HTC business.

Get Simple, Clear, and Focused

This book will help you come up with two or three versions of your core promise to fit each of the different tiers, which you will develop into a legitimate business model.

When done correctly...

1. Your audience sees clear lines of delineation among each offer.
2. They value your expertise.
3. You have one simple sales process to acquire customers and offer them any program level.

What will you experience in your business after you apply this methodology?

1. **Simplicity.** By understanding what activities move the needle, you will know exactly what you need to do to generate those customers and fulfill in a way that makes you feel comfortable and competent.

2. **Clarity.** You will know how to build a bond with your customer so that you can continue serving them and develop that relationship for repeat business.

3. **Focus.** You will know how to make the biggest impact with minimum viable effort.

The Trajectory: Launch, Growth, and Scale

The second element of the HTC model involves the *timing* of your growth. Let's talk about trajectory. In the graphic below, you'll see The Trajectory of business growth in High Ticket Courses broken down into three core phases: **Launch**, **Growth**, and **Scale**.

As you start creating your machine, acquiring customers, and building your lead generation systems, you'll want to figure out how to start growing. Every stage of scaling is meant to give you more time. And if you scale out of order, it will completely break you.

Properly scaling an expert-based business happens in three clear stages. Each stage is designed to get you more time.

TRAJECTORY

Builder
Goal: $10K – $50K/month

PHASE 2: Growth

PHASE 1: Launch

PHASE 3: Scale

Experimenter
Goal: $0 – $10K/month

Leader
Goal: $50K/month and beyond

Phase 1: The Launch Phase (You're the Experimenter)

In Phase 1, the Launch Phase, you're the Experimenter. You'll go from your offer idea to your first $10K per month. (This is not a steadfast rule—it all depends on what your price point is and how many customers it takes to enroll to get to that level.)

In this phase, it's all about validation. This is when you will experience fast growth as you test new offers and ideas. It's critical that you have your lead flow coming in and that you are reaching an audience that constantly wants what you're offering.

Your goal here is to get five paid customers or clients. Your primary focus is to develop the most profitable offer and generate as many enrollment calls as possible. The key activities here are to develop your core messaging and offers that generate a response from an audience who's never heard of you.

You'll notice that in this phase, it's really all about sales. You'll want to test your advertising targets and mediums, your enrollment calls, your lead qualification strategy, your offer structure, and your feedback. And, you'll want to develop your Minimum Viable Funnel layout.

What brings you from the Launch Phase to the next phase—the Growth Phase—is that your offer has been validated. Usually, this means you get past five paid customers, and you're ROI positive. If you get five customers but you're *not* ROI positive, then you can't move past this phase.

This is what it means to be an Experimenter. You have to test things. You have to try new ideas to see what hits and what's going to stick.

Phase 2: The Growth Phase (You're the Builder)

Now that you have found what hits and what sticks, you want to make sure that it actually does stick in the long term. As you move into Phase 2, the Growth Phase, you're the Builder. This is when you'll start to build your foundational structure.

Your goal here is at least three months of consistent $10K–$50K per month. I've seen this happen over and over again. You can go past the validation phase very quickly. Obviously, if you have a relatively expensive high ticket offer (e.g., $5K–$15K), you're going to be blowing past this milestone in a couple of sales. But the most important thing is consistency, no matter your price point.

Your primary focus is making sure that you can fulfill your offers. When you have this dialed in, you develop a downsell offer to increase your closing rate, enroll more of your clients, and expand your revenue opportunities. You'll work on lead-nurturing activities and start list building with lead magnets, low ticket offers, email marketing, and groups.

If you focus on building a solid support structure in Phase 2, you will continue growing even if your primary activities aren't working. For example, if you run into ad issues or your paid ads stop working, you will still have a steady stream of prospective clients who are hyper-qualified.

Now, what brings you from Phase 2 to Phase 3—the Scale Phase—is a steady stream of sales and a growing warm audience. You want to focus on how you will hyper-qualify the leads that are coming into your pipeline. This can take anywhere from 2 to 6 months.

Phase 3: The Scale Phase (You're the Leader)

Phase 3 is when you'll want to start pouring gasoline on the fire. Now you're the Leader, and it's time to scale what is working.

Your goal here is at least three months of no less than $50K per month. *And your primary focus here is really to free your time: Get yourself out of fulfillment and selling as much as possible.*

Develop and perfect your brand building, nurturing, and marketing efforts, so you have an endless warm market. Bring on an advisor to take you off the phones, or hire a coach to support your customers, and decide what you want next. This does not mean you can't get off the phones until you're at Phase 3, but it's easier to add to your team in this phase.

In every one of these stages, you'll hit a capacity at which you cannot produce any more output. You need clear steps to start to remove yourself from the process as you build the right elements in your place.

Which Phase Are You in Right Now?

You need to understand and master the three core phases that High Ticket Course Experts go through as they're building and growing their business model. But, if you want to get into profit fast and have the resources to scale, you need to *start* at Tier 3.

Ask yourself: *Which phase am I in right now?*

Once you know what goes into each phase, you can say, "Here's what it's going to look like when I reach the next tier. Here's what I need to focus on as I start to design this model for myself."

Before you can become a High Ticket Course Expert, though, you need to design your HTC Model. If you master these five elements, your business model will be a success:

1. Avatar
2. Offer
3. Journey
4. Pricing
5. Delivery/Fulfillment

Once you've mastered these five elements, then it's time to think about marketing and scaling. While it's obvious that you need to sell before you scale, many believe you need to market before you sell. That couldn't be further from the truth.

What If You Don't Have a High Ticket Course Ready to Sell?

People think that if they don't have a course created yet that they don't have anything to sell. The truth is you don't need to create your products before you sell them. In fact, you need to sell your services *before* you create a training product, and here's why: The single greatest asset you want to build up in your sales and marketing material is testimonials.

You need to gather case studies of clients who are using your system and your methodology to get results. You might be thinking: *Well, that doesn't make much sense. Then, how do I get those testimonials? How do I get those case studies?*

The answer is by working one-on-one with your first customers. Working one-on-one with them is the best way to make sure they get results and achieve success with your system and methodology. Then, when you're ready to scale to a more hands-off, productized version of your HTC, you can share those results to attract new clients. This is why the High Ticket Courses Model starts at Tier 3, the highest level of service.

You need to do everything in your power to make sure they succeed with your methodology because you're going to be leveraging their success to scale and grow your marketing efforts for your program.

The best part about working with somebody one-on-one is that you need to have absolutely nothing created ahead of time. Let me say that again: *When working one-on-one with somebody, you need absolutely nothing created ahead of time.* All you need is the processing and methodology that you have in your head.

You work one-on-one with them, whether it's in person or remotely through Zoom or Skype calls. You guide them through your process and methodology to help them overcome any obstacles they're facing.

Once you help them get results, you can then start to create your content based on the hurdles they faced. Despite their struggles and needs, you got them results. You can now start to lead with both your success *and* your customer's success.

Don't Create Your Course Before You Sell It

You should never create your course before you sell it. It is bad for you and for your customers. Your customers get the best results when you work one-on-one with them as they encounter each hurdle and milestone. And, it allows you to start getting those testimonials and case studies.

The easiest way to generate demand for your program is to sell based on previous results. Showing people what you have done for others is your most valuable asset to acquire new customers on a regular basis. Why? Because it gives them the ability to see themselves in your customer's shoes.

The reason testimonials, case studies, and client stories are so powerful is that they allow your prospects to see what is possible for them.

NOTE: If you're launching a brand new offer, you'll want to check out highticketcourses.com/bonuses as well as the bonus section of this book. In Bonus #2, you'll find my Perfect Pitch, which is the exact script that I use to get customers and clients without testimonials.

CHAPTER 2

CREATE MESSAGING FOR YOUR IDEAL AVATAR

I've seen far too many people leave money on the table by trying to bang a square peg in a round hole. They're often trying to sell their customers on something they aren't necessarily ready for.

I can't tell you how many people want our done-for-you service (Tier 3), but they're just not financially or mentally in a place where they're ready to take advantage of our agency. Even if they can cut a check, they still have to be in the right place at the right time, in the right frame of mind, and on the right avenue for their business.

Creating the right messaging for your ideal avatar is all about being able to serve more customers by offering them the ability to take the journey that best serves them.

Target the Right Avatar

When I launched my first webinar course, I sold it to the wrong avatar—or ideal customer—inside of my target audience. This was my thought process: *My agency, The Webinar Agency, creates high-converting sales presentations for our customers and for our clients. We've helped at least seven businesses hit the 2-Comma Club Award. I should be able to teach this to people.*

Blindly and with complete ignorance, I thought: *I'm just going to build my course. I'm going to build my education program, drive paid traffic to it, and do my own webinars. I'm going to sell this to my audience.* This was my first attempt at scaling my agency through education.

It was a massive failure.

I generated tens of thousands of dollars in revenue from the initial launch, but when I tried advertising to an audience who'd never heard of me—a cold audience through paid traffic—it flopped. What I wanted was something scalable, and it's next to impossible to scale without paid traffic.

The reason why it didn't work with paid traffic was because of one critical point: Just because I can teach something to someone, doesn't mean they will want to learn how to do it themselves—at least not at a price point that would make it profitable for me. (This also revealed another critical discovery that you'll discover in just a moment.)

I was trying to sell a completely DIY program for $997 with paid ads. For reference, my Tier 3 agency services were $25K. What all of my data was telling me—that I was blind to for months—was that I was marketing to the wrong avatar. My avatar wasn't willing to pay $1,000 to learn how to do a webinar on their own. They knew a webinar was a lot of work, and they didn't want to do it themselves. They needed help ... and lots of it.

It wasn't long before I met with my friend and fellow copywriter, Kevin Rogers. Kevin runs a membership community for freelancers and copywriters. He shows them how to get more clients and level up their copywriting skills.

We did a joint venture (JV) partnership, where he promoted my webinar training program to his community. These copywriters didn't necessarily want to write a webinar for themselves. They wanted to learn how to write webinars for their clients as an additional revenue source. That promotion to Kevin's audience went extremely well. We ended up closing approximately $30K in sales.

Because of the JV promotion to Kevin Rogers' audience, I decided to make an avatar pivot, and I focused on teaching other people how to create million-dollar webinars as a business they could market to others. And *that* took off like wildfire.

The key lesson is this: You may have the perfect offer but the wrong audience. Be flexible with whom you can serve. Most people who teach avatar design mislead their customers, whether intentionally or unintentionally. And to be quite honest, it's catastrophic.

You could have the perfect offer targeting the wrong avatar and go completely broke because of it. That's exactly what happened to me when I started marketing my webinar course.

Closest to the Conversion Hole

I want to introduce you to what I call the Closest to the Conversion Hole methodology—the simplest and most powerful avatar exercise and explanation that I've ever seen out there.

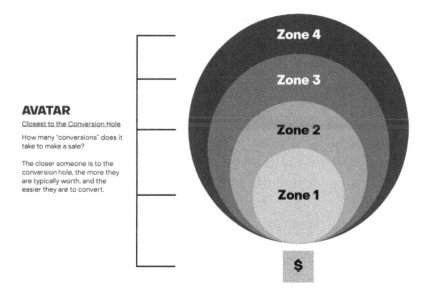

AVATAR

Closest to the Conversion Hole

How many "conversions" does it take to make a sale?

The closer someone is to the conversion hole, the more they are typically worth, and the easier they are to convert.

This is all about asking yourself: *How many conversions does it take to make a sale?* The gold square at the bottom with the dollar sign is your ultimate conversion hole—the sale. This is when somebody says, "Yes, Mr. or Ms. Expert, I believe in your promise, and I'm willing to pay you for your expertise." The closer someone is to the conversion hole, the more they are typically worth, and the easier they are to convert.

Every time that I say "conversion," I'm not necessarily referring to a sale. I'm talking about a belief that brings a potential customer closer to buying into your product. The further somebody is away from your conversion hole (i.e., Zones 3 and 4), the more they have to be educated and sold on your product being the right fit for them.

Example: Stock Market Investing

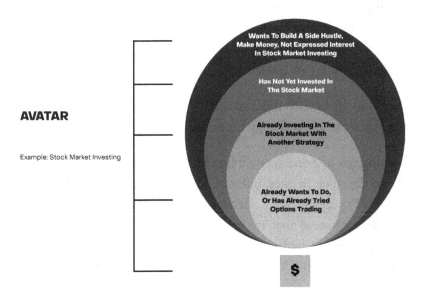

AVATAR

Example: Stock Market Investing

Imagine that you've got a High Ticket Program that teaches people how to make money through options trading. The best odds for your success would be to target the person who is closest to the conversion hole.

Ask yourself: *Who would most likely be interested in my options trading course?* In most cases, the answer is going to be the person who has tried options trading and failed. That's the person who is closest to your conversion hole and therefore most likely to buy into your product or service.

So, in the case of stock market investing, somebody who already wants to do options trading, or who has already tried options trading and failed, would need the least amount of education on your methodology. This is because they already know that they want to do options trading, and they've already bought into why options trading is right for them, but they tried a previous system that failed. So now, your avatar is laser-targeted because these people need very little convincing on your offer. They are in Zone 1, closest to the conversion hole.

Your only focus with this avatar is: Why is your unique methodology the right methodology for them?

Moving out to Zone 2, you'll find somebody who is already investing in the stock market, but with another strategy (e.g., day trading, ETFs, crypto, etc.). Here, you're targeting somebody who's already convinced that investing in the stock market is the best way for them to make money. So, you'll need to make two conversions before they become a client: You need to convince them on options, and you need to convince them that your particular options methodology is the right path for them.

Now to go even further out to Zone 3, you'll find somebody who has not yet invested in the stock market. They know about the stock market, but they're not yet taking action. So, you have three conversions to get this client. First, you have to tell them that the best way for them to have success is by investing in the stock market, then it's through options, then it's through your specific options trading system.

The further out you go, the more conversion conversations you need to have.

On the widest spectrum (Zone 4), your prospect wants to build a side hustle to make money, and they've not yet expressed interest in stock market investing. So now you have to start by saying, "Listen, you need to really pay attention to the stock market if you want to make money. And here's why." Then, "You have to really pay attention to options trading." Then, "Here's why you should pay attention to my methodology of options trading." That's a pretty far reach.

Now, this is going to be the largest audience, but these are not necessarily people who are going to take action right now because they don't have any urgency. The timing is off if your offer isn't even on their radar.

As you get closer to the hole, your messaging becomes more and more relevant, and your conversation gets dialed in. But it's all about making sure you're talking to the right avatar.

Focus on Zone 1, or maybe Zones 1 and 2, but stay as close to the conversion hole as possible.

This example is in the hard ROI, make money niche, so if you have a soft offer, you may be thinking, *This won't work for me because my offer isn't about ROI.* So let's take a look at another example.

Example: Personal Development (PD)

Let's look at personal development for a moment. If your offer is teaching people Neuro-Linguistic Programming (NLP) tactics for personal development, law of attraction, or any other soft offer, who do you want to target first? Somebody who's never heard of NLP? Or somebody who has already tried NLP for personal development and failed?

You guessed it. The one who has tried and failed.

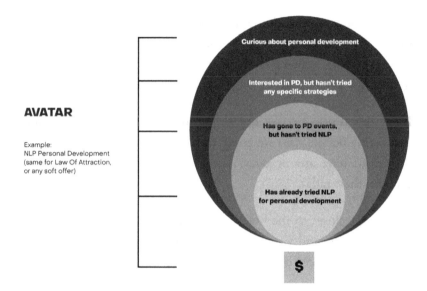

AVATAR

Example:
NLP Personal Development
(same for Law Of Attraction,
or any soft offer)

After hundreds of consulting calls, I can predict what my personal development clients are going to say when we start dialing in their avatar and offer. I'll say, "Tell me who you want to serve," and 90% of the time, they'll say, "People who want to make their life better."

Then I'll ask, "What is your offer?" And they'll say, "I want to teach Law of Attraction and NLP." They don't realize they have to educate and warm up their Zone 4 prospects. Otherwise, it's like walking up to people who are only curious about PD, LOA, or NLP and saying, "I'm going to show you how to live your best life ever!"

By doing this, you're missing the boat. You really have to change your "who" and go after the people who have already gone to the seminars, who have already read the books, who already know the language and terminology. For example, look for people who have already tried NLP or the law of attraction—people who want to take it to the next level. This is where you want to start. Begin by explaining to them why they failed before and why your methodology is the right fit for them.

Urgency Drives Conversion

You've got to get your avatar dialed in. If you put your focus on somebody who has tried and failed, I guarantee that you will speak to your perfect customer, or at least to the person who's willing to say yes and give you money right away.

Develop a closest-to-the-hole mentality. This could quite possibly be one of the biggest takeaways that you can have from this book.

Get this wrong and one of two things will happen as you start driving paid traffic into your funnel:

1. Nobody will respond. Or...
2. The people who do respond will be tire kickers.

The easiest way to spot this is if your advertising costs are through the roof.

The biggest mistake that I see when people are creating their avatar is that they choose someone who is in Zone 3 or Zone 4, not realizing that those people take the longest to convert and are the least likely to convert right away.

People in Zones 3 and 4 are too far away; they have to be convinced of too many things. And this is going to show up in your opt-in conversion rate. It's going to show up in your lead quality. It's going to show up in people not applying to work with you because you're speaking to somebody who's too far away from urgency.

You want people who are experiencing urgency around their struggles because that sense of urgency will drive their decision to work with you—in turn, increasing your conversions.

The Chet Holmes Buyers Pyramid

Here's how I got this wrong and how it cost me dearly.

When we were running paid traffic just to grow our agency, we focused on this idea of "Give value first, then make the offer second." And what did we do? Well, we're The Webinar Agency, so we had to run long-form webinars. This worked well for many of my clients, but it just wasn't working for us.

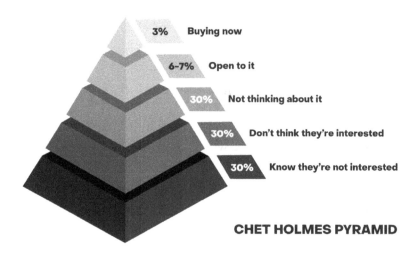

- 3% Buying now
- 6-7% Open to it
- 30% Not thinking about it
- 30% Don't think they're interested
- 30% Know they're not interested

CHET HOLMES PYRAMID

I could generate leads, but it was very expensive to generate a sale. The reason why was because I was trying to educate my market, and this is a huge misconception in the marketplace. We all think that we need to educate our market, and while a little bit of education can be good or even necessary, I was trying to educate that Zone 3 and Zone 4 customer.

Applying the "closest to the hole" mentality, I was having conversations with people who were furthest from the conversion hole. The longer it took to convert, the more money I needed to spend. This left me bleeding time and burning money. I don't want the same thing to happen to you, which is why it's so important for you to get this concept.

Another way to look at this by studying the Chet Holmes Buyers Pyramid. In his book *The Ultimate Sales Machine*[2], he talks about this buyers pyramid of the people in your marketplace. There's a segment of them that are interested in buying right now. There's another segment of people who are open to it. Then there's another segment of people who don't think they're interested, and then those who know that they're not interested.

Right now you've got 3-4% of your market (the top of the pyramid) considering buying either your offer or a competitor's offer. And there's another 6-7% (the next level down) who are open to it. Meaning, if they're presented with the right offer and the right opportunity, they will take action. The remaining 90% of your market (comprising the largest part of the pyramid) are not your target. Either they aren't considering your offer, or they are not interested at all.

---

[2] Chet Holmes, *The Ultimate Sales Machine: Turbocharge Your Business with Relentless Focus on 12 Key Strategies* (New York, NY: Portfolio, 2007), p. 64.

So the number one mistake to avoid when you look at this buyers pyramid is trying to capture the entire market. You don't want to try to capture all five segments with one message, which is what most people do. This is exactly what I did when I was struggling to grow my webinar agency.

This usually ends with the message targeting the bottom portion of the pyramid—those who are least likely to respond because they know that they're not interested. They're not even connected to a problem you solve or an opportunity you offer. Or if they are connected, they've already told themselves that they are not going to entertain any offers, which makes them completely unlikely to respond.

This is exactly what I did wrong. I was trying to educate my broadest market instead of focusing on the narrower, yet still quite large, market of people ready to buy my services and my programs immediately. The further down the pyramid that you are, the longer it takes to convert and the more money it costs to acquire.

It's best to avoid having to educate—and even motivate—consumers as to why it's important to invest in themselves. The person who is actively looking for your solution is someone who already knows why it's important. They're already part of your world, they speak your language, and they're actively looking to level up their game.

They know they must invest to find a solution to accelerate and multiply their success.

When all of your messaging targets your ideal avatar, your conversion rates will not only increase but you'll also reduce the time spent acquiring new clients. And you might even hit a few "holes-in-one."

CHAPTER 3

CREATE YOUR POWER OFFER

Michael, one of my High Ticket Courses clients, came to me with an idea and wanted market validation. We got on a call, and I asked him what he was thinking. His message was: "I help college students achieve better grades through my unique study methods, where they can learn how to retain more information."

I think his Big Promise was "Get at least one letter grade higher than what you were getting." I was concerned he would run into problems, so I wanted him to explain more.

I asked, "Have you launched your Power Offer? Have you started generating any leads for this?"

Michael said, "Yes, but I'm running into an issue."

I said, "What's the issue?" though I already knew what the issue was before he told me. I wanted him to tell me.

He shared that his issues were twofold:

First, he was pursuing broke college students who may have from $30K to $60K in loans. They didn't have money to spend on training and probably also lacked the desire to invest any more in themselves. Even though his promise was the tangible result of getting better grades, his prospects either weren't willing to put in the work or weren't able to pay for his services. So, after talking to a student who liked his course, he would often hear, "If I'm going to do this, then my parents have to pay for it."

This further delayed any conversions because there were now *two* decision makers. He wasn't having any success. I dug deeper: "All right, man. Tell me a little bit more about your situation. Obviously, the market you're going after is one you're passionate about. But, it hasn't been viable for you as a business model. So tell me, what's your secret sauce?"

Michael started telling me all about his methodology for studying. And then I started asking him some other questions like, "Who else can benefit from the study method you came up with?"

And he suggested, "Well, anybody can benefit from it," which I politely accepted.

One of the ideas I had for him (which I wanted him to discover for himself) was to find an alternative market with greater potential. I asked, "If anybody can benefit from it, then what if you were able to take this same method and apply it to somebody who was willing and able to pay for it?"

"Well, I don't really know who is willing *and able* to pay for a study method," he said.

"Ask yourself: Who else would find value in your direct, tangible result of better grades by learning how to study better?"

He identified a market of professionals who have to take licensing exams. They have to study for these really difficult tests that can affect their careers and incomes significantly.

Then the question was, "Do you feel they'd benefit from applying your study methodology to their licensing exams?"

He thought it through: These people are professionals. They probably have a family, and they likely don't have as much time to study, but it's important and valuable for them to pass these exams to get new certifications or updated licenses in order to advance their careers.

Because it would directly lead to a promotion and greater prosperity, the professional would be both willing and able. So, we adjusted the messaging for this new target market to show them how his learning methodology would help them pass their exam in less time and get a promotion.

The more you can attach your offer to a significant, measurable result, the more value your prospects will attach to your service. This will multiply their desire to engage you at premium prices.

Never Go Hungry for Leads Again

Even if you plan out the best model and develop the best program in the world that gets great results for clients, it'll be unsuccessful if you can't create demand.

To avoid this, let me introduce you to what may be one of the most powerful weapons you can ever have in your arsenal.

I want to help you create what I call the "Power Offer." My intention for you is to take action with this, right now. My clients who launched their Power Offers to their network immediately won business from them. I promise you—it has worked dozens upon dozens of times.

Recently, I hosted a training for my friend Rob Kosberg to teach his audience my Power Offer framework.

Rob runs a company called Best Seller Publishing which helps authors launch their books. Even though Rob and I have known each other for years, this was the first time he really grasped the potential of my Power Offer framework. He decided to test his own Power Offer with his audience and was surprised at the results.

In Rob's words, here's what happened:

> "I used it for a simple offer that I made. With one single Facebook post, **I sold out 20 spots of a $6K program. That's $120K in sales from one single Power Offer.** I love your framework!"

I want to walk you through this quickly. This one tactic is what opened the floodgates for me when I was really struggling to get leads, set appointments, and talk to people who wanted to buy my High Ticket program. Once I launched this Power Offer, our cost per application dropped by 90%!

If you understand how to use the Power Offer, **you'll never go hungry for leads again.** You'll know how to create demand for any offer. And, you'll know how to communicate clearly and precisely to get people excited about what you're offering. If they're not getting excited, you just keep revising your Power Offer until people do start responding—just like Rob's audience did.

This is sales. This is not marketing.

This is why I recommend you start with sales first and then marketing. We don't want you getting tripped up with all the gobbledygook of lead magnets and all the complexity of both technology and strategy.

Start with your offer. Then work backward.

This works for private messages, for people in your network who might be interested in what you have to offer, for social media channels, for your email list, and for your customer list. It doesn't matter. It works. It also works anywhere you have a live audience (on a stage, online in a Zoom conference, etc.). And the framework is very simple.

The Power Offer Framework

Here is an example that opened up the floodgates for me and showed me the power of a compelling offer:

Call out the Avatar: *Attention course creators, coaches, and experts.*

Offer a benefit: *If I offer to* **(1)** *build you a high-converting sales webinar with a super-fast turnaround (about 24 hours)* **(2)** *without you needing to worry about what to say, or how to say it,* **(3)** *so you can fill your courses and programs now ...*

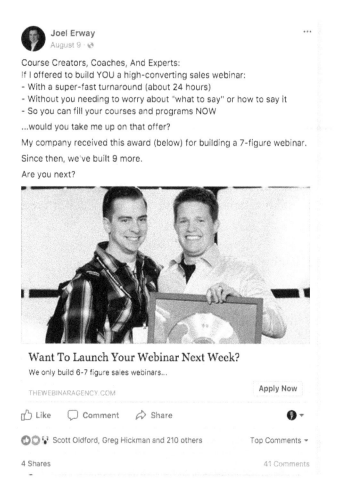

Ask: *Would you take me up on that offer?*

(Optional) Provide proof or authority: *My company received this award below for building a seven-figure webinar and since then we've built nine more.*

Ask: *Are you next?*

How to Craft Your Own Power Offer

Call out the Avatar: *Attention* _____.

Offer a benefit: *If I offer to* (1)_____

(2) *without you* _____

(3) *so you* _____
_____ (use as many or as few points as you need)

Ask: *Would you take me up on that offer?*

(Optional) Provide proof or authority:
_____
_____
_____

Ask: *Are you next?*

I want to challenge you. Create your own Power Offer, and start posting it in your various communication channels or in private messages to stir up interest and desire for whatever you offer.

This fast-action activity is going to create demand.

If you want step-by-step help to create your own Power Offer, I've put together a workshop specifically to show you how to do it. Go to PowerOfferWorkshop.com.

Brad's Story

Brad had a successful coaching program that helped people learn options trading, but he struggled to get a consistent flow of new leads coming in month after month.

He had tried all sorts of different marketing tactics, including ascension-based funnels with free lead magnets. Frustrated because his efforts weren't producing results, he joined the HTC mentorship program to learn to scale his High Ticket offer.

The Power Offer was the game changer for Brad.

Once he knew how to construct an offer that appealed to his ideal Zone 1 avatar, everything changed. It made his Facebook and YouTube ads convert. It brought the right people to him.

Once he got this dialed in, he was booking calls at $30 each and converted those leads at nearly a 50% conversion rate on a $3,000 coaching offer.

After his first month, he generated more than $20K in revenue, which had never happened before.

Brad now experiences consistent, multiple-five-figure months, and he's thrilled because he loves his clients. They are his ideal clients.

And the best part?

Because of his ongoing success, Brad's wife was able to fully retire, which means they get to spend more time together as a family, raising their two young, very active boys.

When he harnessed the power of developing and leading with a Power Offer, Brad started seeing consistent sales, *and* he got his life back.

Questions to Help You Write Your Power Offer

Your offer will depend on your ideal avatar and your ability to deliver. Just because you're experiencing consistent sales doesn't mean you won't risk burnout. Before you create your Power Offer, ask yourself the following questions:

- What does my customer already know, want, and need?
- If my customer has tried and failed, how can I specifically help them?
- How can I simplify my promise so that it makes sense?
- Am I using too many jargon words that nobody understands?
- What are the micro and macro milestones that I can help my customers reach as fast as possible?
- How long would it take me to help them achieve a micro/macro result? How long would it take them to achieve it on their own?
- Are they willing to pay for a solution? Are others already paying for a solution?
- How do I make it so this offer "feels" real? Can I recreate an experience for them?

Once you've answered these questions, begin to craft an offer that takes each of the following elements into consideration:

1. A Clear and Simple Promise
2. Immediacy/Instant Involvement
3. Maximum Value
4. Tangible

Your prospect needs to be able to understand exactly what you're talking about when you make your core promise. Make sure your language is connected to a Zone 1 customer, and don't oversell it. Keep it clear and simple.

You want to give your prospects a sense of immediacy. They're looking for instant involvement as well as a projected timeline. They need to be able to sense and feel when they will achieve a particular result. Don't make an offer without a time element attached to it.

Your offer should solve problems your prospect is willing to pay for—something that's necessary for them to move forward. Move them away from the pain they're in and provide maximum value.

Finally, the results of your offer need to be tangible. Your prospect should be able to imagine themselves experiencing the benefits of your offer without further explanation from you.

There's a balance here. This is the dance. You need to really focus on what you can deliver and what you can promise. So many people miss this. Ultimately, you need to craft the perfect offer for YOU.

CHAPTER 4

SET UP YOUR MINIMAL VIABLE FUNNEL

N ovice entrepreneurs often ask, "What is the funnel that you used to grow your business?" You really only need one type of funnel until you're well into Phase 3 of the HTC model: The Minimum Viable Funnel (MVF).

The goal here is meant to drive high ticket sales. If you're doing a strict return on ad spend, your cost-per-sale is going to be the lowest with this funnel, because you're targeting people who actively have a problem and are searching for a solution.

The length of this funnel is short and immediate. Ultimately, you really want them to just book a call. This funnel uses a mini webinar—a 10- to 12-minute presentation that gives them the "need to know" information: "Here's what you need to know. Let's hop on the phone and see if we can make a deal right now."

The message here is focused on providing an immediate benefit and value in exchange for your program. You're making that offer and showing them the roadmap of what it looks like to work with you.

Use this funnel during Phases 1 and 2. This will get you to $30K–$50K per month on average (sometimes a lot more, depending on the market), so it's going to be sufficient for most experts.

Ask yourself:

- What type of funnel would I rather go through if I were in a buying mode?
- What would I rather create as a business owner to attract customers and clients? Longer or shorter funnels?

Validate Your Offer

The Monopoly Rule: Until you validate your offer, "_Do not pass go. Do not collect $200._"

If you can't validate your offer, nothing else in business matters. You can attract all the people in the world onto your email list, but if they don't want or need your offer, all else fails. You validate your offer by acquiring customers with the Minimum Viable Funnel (MVF).

The MVF gives you a framework to naturally lead someone who's never heard of you to pay you money for a program or service.

You will use the MVF to identify the three key criteria to qualify them:

1. They have a time-sensitive need.

2. They believe in your process and methodology as a solution.

3. They are willing and able to pay for help.

That is all they need to be qualified.

They have a problem they are ready to solve, they believe in your process and methodology as a solution, and they are willing and able to pay for help.

> **What they don't need is a long webinar—a painful sales conversation that's disguised as a strategy session.**

A strategy session is a form of marketing ... educating the prospect on your process or methodology. But the prospect hasn't been pre-sold yet.

Make the Damn Offer

With the MVF, the whole premise is to use a mini webinar to lead with the offer in order to pre-sell the prospect (a sales action), instead of trying to acquire leads and then make an offer (a marketing action).

Start by making the damn offer (MTDO). This is the shortcut when you're starting out. You have to engineer an offer that people want. If you can't do that, and if you can't promote it, nothing else matters.

The principle here is to focus on validating your core offer and generating sales *before* descending to the lower tiers and expanding to the rest of the buyers pyramid. Craft an offer that targets the top 10% of the market: Those who are open to buying now if they're presented with an offer that makes sense to them. Give them a compelling offer and a clear solution.

This group is closest to the conversion hole, which means a shorter funnel. This simplifies your focus to identify what really matters. You get instant feedback, which is both good and bad. If people are saying that they don't want the offer, you've got some valuable feedback—it might not be translating into a sale, but it tells you that you need to pivot.

Start small before scaling. This allows you to create micro-tests before you start pumping more ad dollars in and generating other content that will not translate into more revenue.

MTDO allows you to test with paid traffic, which is the holy grail. If you don't have a list, this is huge. Ultimately, you want to move into paid traffic because this is where you're able to grow quickly and maintain a lifestyle where you're not on a constant marketing hamster wheel.

This also targets premium buyers who value their time over their money, allowing you to charge a premium price point. Your cost per acquisition is also going to be the lowest.

The Client/Customer Acquisition Process

The MVF is designed in five simple steps:

1. Power Offer

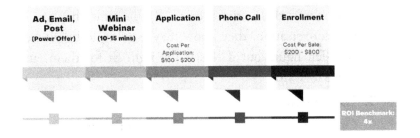

THE CUSTOMER ACQUISITION PROCESS

Here is your message where you're going to be making the damn offer–what I call your Power Offer. You make that promise and get people interested. Once you get them to raise their hand, they're going to give you their email and watch a short presentation.

2. Mini Webinar

On average, these are 10-15 minutes long. The goal of the mini webinar is just to give them an overview of your process. This is what they need to understand to make a yes-or-no buying decision. The primary goal of the mini webinar is to reveal your methodology so they can answer the question: Do I believe this methodology is the right way for me to achieve results?

3. Application

If they watch your mini webinar and connect with it, they fill out an application where they're going to pre-qualify themselves and tell you a little bit more about their situation, so you can determine if they're a good fit or not.

4. **Phone Call**

They will schedule a phone call where you have a quick enrollment conversation. I'm not going to call this a "strategy session" because they've already been presold throughout this entire process. By the time they get to this conversation, they know they're going to be pitched an offer, figure out if this is the right fit for them, and move forward.

5. **Enrollment**

Only enroll them if you can confidently say, "Working together is a grand slam, and here's why ..." At that point, you simply show them the roadmap and collect payment if they are a good fit. Your benchmark during this entire process is a bare minimum of 4X return on ad spend.

Step 1 of the MVF: The Power Offer Ad

Right now, you are targeting the top 10% in the market who are closest to the conversion hole. You're being direct and making them an offer by attracting them into your world with your promise.

Remember my example of a successful Power Offer in the last chapter? I want to show you how that offer fits into the MVF.

My headline: *Want to Launch Your Webinar Next Week?*

My subheading: *We only build 6-7 figure sales webinars...*

My Power Offer ad copy:

Course Creators, Coaches, and Experts:

If I offered to build YOU a high-converting sales webinar:

- *With a super-fast turnaround (about 24 hours)*
- *Without you needing to worry about "what to say" or how to say it*
- *So you can fill your courses and programs NOW*

…would you take me up on that offer?

My company received this award (below) for building a 7-figure webinar.

Since then, we've built 9 more.

Are you next?

I used a photo of me with Russell Brunson, co-founder of ClickFunnels. We were standing together as I accepted my "Two Comma Club" award for achieving at least $1M through a single sales funnel. It received hundreds of reactions, comments, and shares and generated massive revenue. I would argue that the main reason it performed so well is that it deeply resonated with my audience. (Go back to The Power Offer Framework in Chapter 3 to see a screenshot.)

This was my launchpad.

It's a very simple framework. However, it takes a lot of mental bandwidth and an understanding of your marketplace to be able to come up with this offer while still being able to create compelling ad copy, framed in a way that your audience understands.

This caused me to go from dreading strategy sessions in sales calls to actually enjoying the conversations because these people knew that we were going to be talking about my program.

Ask yourself:

- What is my core promise?
- Is anyone else making similar claims?
- How am I different from them?
- What does my avatar—who's already tried and failed—know?

If you read this copy from my Power Offer ad again, you will see that all of these questions are answered, either directly or indirectly. We were building skeleton webinars with the core elements of what they wanted.

Step 2 of the MVF: The Mini Webinar

In Step 2 of the MVF, you've got their name and email, and they've expressed interest in your offer. At this point, they're attracted to your promise.

There are two burning questions in your prospect's mind: *How does it work? And will it work for me?*

This is important.

You can use a mini webinar to give them an overview of your process, how you work, and how you help people achieve your promise. This is your automated sales rep because here's the secret: If they believe in your process and methodology, they will convince themselves that it will work for them, and you don't need to do any "selling."

Potential clients don't want to be spending a whole lot of time sitting in on a 60- to 75-minute-long webinar, enduring a whole song and dance. These people want the bottom line. They value their time more than their money. They simply want to know exactly what it is you've got to offer. They'll figure out for themselves if your methodology is right for them.

And then, they want to make a yes-or-no decision right away—or very soon. At my agency, it was not unheard of to close deals for $10K, $15K, or $30K within just 24 hours of somebody first being introduced to us. They value their time more than their money, even when making a financial decision.

This should be a big "Aha!" moment because the vast majority of people in the digital marketing space who have a typical sales funnel will run a long-form webinar or a free lead-magnet funnel. They create a one- to two-hour-long webinar. They invite people to go watch it. Then at the end, they invite them to book a call, or they invite them to make a purchase. This was the type of funnel I was running for a long time, where I was selling an $8,000 webinar-group-coaching program.

I was having a heck of a time trying to make it work. And I didn't figure out the problem until I realized that my audience—my ideal avatar—just wasn't seeing the offer. They were learning about my stuff, but because they valued their time more than their money, they would drop off the webinar before I made the offer.

Once I realized this, I flipped the whole script on its head. I led with the offer. Then, I gave them the basic, minimum, need-to-know information, *and the game changed entirely.*

This revelation is why I created the mini webinar, which is on average about a 10- to 15-minute, *short* presentation that attracts ideal, qualified candidates and gives them the summarized, need-to-know information.

The people you attract through ads don't have to register for a date and time to sign up for this webinar. It's just a prerecorded video that has the fluff cut out of it.

To be clear, **the mini webinar is not really designed to educate them a whole lot. It's designed to get them excited about the opportunity, show them what your process is, show them your methodology, and then invite them to take the next step forward.**

Ask yourself:

- What has my audience already experienced with other similar offers?
- How is my offer and promise different?
- What is my unique mechanism?
- How is my delivery mechanism explained?
- Do I have a clear process to explain how to get my defined outcome?
- Does this make me sound like everyone else, or do I stand out?
- Is my offer believable?

Step 3 of the MVF: The Application

After watching your mini webinar, a percentage of people will inquire about taking the next step. They will want to speak with you about this opportunity.

But, in order to schedule a time to speak with you, they must give you more information about themselves to prove they are serious candidates.

The goal here is to screen your leads, find out who is the best fit for your program, and automate your qualification process.

If someone is not a good fit for you, you'll have a good indication before you get on the phone with them. And this will continue to evolve as you develop your ideal customer.

When first developing this form, less is more.

Too many questions will scare off your leads. Shoot for no more than five questions. As you start collecting responses and having enrollment calls, you can determine whether or not you need to revise your questions or add more.

The key is to ask yourself: "What do I need to know about my ideal customer that clearly identifies them as being a great fit for me?"

And an even better question to ask yourself is, "What questions can I ask that will tell me if someone is *not* a perfect fit?" Identify who your non-ideal customer is.

Once you know who *isn't* a good fit for you, you can use the flip side of this person to help you identify the perfect customer.

Create your exclusion list. Be the boss, take control, and get clear on who you're not willing to work with.

Everyone's assessment form will be different. But here are a few of my favorite questions to ask:

1. What is your current situation? (Read: Where are you in life/business right now?)
2. What is your desired situation? (Read: Where do you want to be?)
3. What do you feel is holding you back from getting to that desired situation? (Read: What problems are you experiencing?)
4. What have you already tried to do to solve this problem?
5. Why is NOW the time to get help with your situation? (Read: How urgent is this problem to solve?)

Getting the answers to these questions will tell you immediately how serious the lead is about getting your help to transform their current situation.

And it will help you direct the phone call and enrollment conversation.

BONUS TIP: If you want to further qualify your leads before you get on the phone with them, you can choose to follow up with them via text or email before your scheduled call with what I call the **3-Question Pre-Close**.

After someone submits their application, I will follow up with the following message:

"Hey (NAME), I just received your assessment form. I've got a few follow-up questions based on what I see. Mind if I send them over?"

Then, I will ask these three questions before I get on a call with the lead.

If you choose to use this strategy, your closing rate will skyrocket because the lead will be framed as strong as possible for a sale.

It reduces any tension that might have been present on the enrollment call if these questions hadn't been answered.

Here is the 3-Question Pre-Close:

1. Why do you feel my methodology will work for you?
2. Are you looking to get support now or later?
3. Are you able to invest in getting a solution now?

Assuming they say "yes" to the final question, they're 95% of the way sold on your offer program. Your scheduled enrollment call will be a breeze.

Steps 4 & 5 of the MVF: The Phone Call and Enrollment

Steps 4 and 5 go hand in hand. You're going to get on the phone with your prospect, and assuming they're your ideal candidate, you're going to enroll them into your program.

This is more of a Q&A call to determine if you are compatible with each other. Your prospect should be pre-sold before getting on a call with you. They should already be familiar with your process, and they should know an offer will be discussed on the call.

Do not bait and switch them like in a typical strategy session. Treat these people as professionals—the way you would like to be treated.

As you listen to their situation, exude confidence in your ability to help them. You shouldn't do any educating on the call; instead, tell them how you see your program applying to their specific situation.

One of my favorite ways to do this is with the "Home Run" affirmation, which is: "Thanks for sharing more info about your situation. Based on everything you've told me, I have complete confidence in my ability to help you. In fact, this offer will be a home run for you, and here's why." Then, explain why you know your offer will help them get results.

This is not a strategy session, and you don't have to follow a sales script. You just need to listen, affirm, and enroll.

High ticket clients need a phone call to enroll. You might be tempted to do "automatic" sales so that you never have to speak to clients on the phone. For that to work, you would need to be an expert marketer. You would need to know copywriting, how to create an email sequence, and how to create, manage, and scale ads. And you would need to hire someone to handle chargebacks and refunds. None of this is necessary with the MVF.

The Minimum Viable Funnel is your fastest and simplest way to generate customers and clients for a High Ticket offer. If you can't commit to the MVF, you shouldn't commit to this business at all.

CHAPTER 5

OUTLINE YOUR CUSTOMER JOURNEY

*"Anyone can steer the ship, but it takes a leader
to chart the course."*

—John C. Maxwell

It's your job to map out the whole trip people will take through your world of expertise so they can see the hurdles, the opportunities, and the gains.

When I was selling my first High Ticket coaching program back in 2016, I sold it for between $5K and $8K, without a journey. It's possible to sell these coaching programs as tools, which is what I was doing. I was teaching people how to create a high-converting webinar, and I was coaching them through it.

These people came in already committed, saying, "Yes, I want a webinar. I understand why webinars are great, and I want your help to create one." And once these people got done with the program, they said, "Okay, great. Thanks for the webinar. I'll see you later!" There was no next step for them.

I never positioned this program as a stepping stone to a greater result.

It was a broken business model.

Not only was it broken, but it was also taking us longer to teach them than to build out the webinar ourselves. Rather than spending six, eight, or ten weeks coaching, we could have focused on doing it for them, which would have saved a lot of time and generated far better results.

This is what happens when you build a broken business model—when you don't design a customer journey around your course, and you try to just productize an agency offer that isn't necessarily worth productizing.

It would have been better for me to sell my done-for-you services at the same price that I was selling my coaching program because it was taking us less time to fulfill these offers.

The moral of the story here is to build a journey around your offer. Never get pigeonholed as selling just a tool, because tools are like bandaids. You want somebody coming into your world understanding that there's more to the story than your offer.

A customer journey is important because:

- It gives YOU clarity on how you can help them by defining your Macro Milestone and Micro Milestones.

- It gives your customers trust and confidence in the plan to achieve their goal.

- It creates lines of delineation for what you need to include so you don't overpromise or cannibalize your offer.

- It creates new opportunities for growth and new ways your customers can work with you.

- It gives you more ideas for how to attract your ideal customers.

- It shows them all the steps in the process, and it ties them to a greater goal.

The HTC Customer Journey

First, we have our **Big Promise**. We will help our clients launch their High Ticket Course, get interested leads in the first 14-30 days, make their first sale within six weeks, and build the foundation for a $10K–$30K/month High Ticket Course and Coaching business.

Then we have **Onboarding** where they reach the first three milestones: identify their money market; identify their idea, minimum viable offer, and model; and develop their one- to two-sentence Power Offer.

By the end of that, they're going to hit a major milestone, which is having a clear **Power Offer**. Then we go into the next three milestones: develop their mini webinar, technical setup, and launch their Power Offer.

Now they've hit the **Launch** milestone, and they move into the next three: generate their first leads, generate their first applications and phone calls, and close their first sale. Boom! **Sales Closed**. Finally: Optimize, rinse, and repeat until they're comfortable.

By the end of this journey, they've got the foundations built for a $10K- to $30K-per-month High Ticket Course and Coaching business. In a nutshell, we want them to hit certain milestones within a 4-week period:

> **Week 1:** Develop their avatar and create their Power Offer
>
> **Week 2:** Create their mini webinar
>
> **Week 3:** Launch their offer
>
> **Weeks 4-12:** Optimize and enroll

Here's what our Milestone Plan looks like from a visual standpoint:

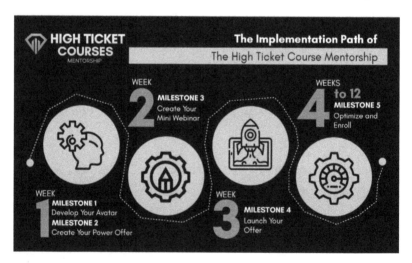

This roadmap shows them what they need to do every step along the way to get the result. The Big Promise that you're leading with is super important. You do not need to create a graphic for it—you just need to create your outline of customer success milestones. This is what they are going to need to see to have confidence in your ability to deliver your core promise.

How to Avoid My Mistake

Here's the secret to having long-term clients and customers with High Ticket Courses: Make sure that what you are designing not only solves a current problem but also *introduces new problems.*

For example, when someone enters my world and launches a High Ticket Course, the major milestone that we help them achieve is validating and selling their High Ticket Course to an audience who's never heard of them before.

That alone comes with its own set of challenges that I help them solve, either in our agency or in our mentorship program.

Once they complete that goal, I know from experience they are going to run into a number of different problems, such as:

- Fulfillment issues at scale
- Sales systems at scale (Do I hire a salesperson? If so, what's the best way to do that?)
- Marketing systems at scale
- Do I create low ticket offers?
- Do I create a podcast, blog, etc.?
- Customer service issues at scale
- And more ...

Some of these problems I have expertise in solving. Others I refer out to other experts who are better suited to help them.

The key point is to make sure you are designing a journey that continues past your initial promise, so your customers and clients will want to keep paying you for your advice and support.

Otherwise, you'll be churning through clients and customers, always on that cycle of needing to acquire new ones to stay in business.

As you design your program, ask yourself: *What am I struggling with and where do I need to really focus my attention to make sure that my avatar is following that map?* Understand what your avatar wants and give them a clear path to getting it. Those are two of the three big things that you need to have success. The third thing is making sure you show up every day.

Defining Your Own Customer Journey

Ask yourself:

1. What is the ultimate END RESULT (Macro Goal) I'm promising someone? For example, when they complete my program, what will happen or what will they become?
2. After someone completes payment, what is the first thing that will happen? What next?
3. How can I separate my Milestones into Micro Goals?

This is how you can develop that customer journey, and explain it to your customers and audience so they know and trust that you can deliver the goods. This is all about trust and keeping them on the right path. Nobody wants to follow a blind leader.

You can tell them all of the instructions verbally, but they're not going to trust themselves to remember it. They might second-guess themselves. But if you give them a map and clear, step-by-step instructions that they can't screw up, you've built that trust factor with them.

Let's dig a little deeper with a quick exercise:

1. Define your **Big Promise (Macro Goal)** that happens when someone completes your program. Finish this statement: "By the end of the program, my customer will _____."

2. List out all of the **Milestones** from the moment someone enrolls to when they complete the program.

3. Create steps to achieve and complete each **Milestone (Micro Goal).**

4. Review your finished document and ask yourself:

   a. What are the most valuable Micro Goals in my program?

   b. Am I delivering too much? Too little?

   c. Are my goals and steps realistic within the time frame I'm giving them? Too much, too soon? Overwhelm?

   d. Do I have a "Next Step" for them to take after they've accomplished the Macro Goal?

After you've worked through this exercise, ask yourself these questions:

- Do I have any Micro Goals that can serve as a Macro Goal? (Meaning: Will people pay for a solution to a Micro Goal?)

- Do I have a journey, or next step, for what happens at the end of the Macro Goal?

- What are the major obstacles that I can foresee people running into even with my help? How can I help them overcome those obstacles?

If you want your customers and clients to sell your program for you through glowing testimonials, map out their journey for them. Work through these questions. Your answers will become the foundation for a program that gets your clients the best possible results.

As you think through all of your client's potential obstacles and implement as many solutions as possible, you create an unmatched customer journey that will develop raving fans and customers for life.

CHAPTER 6

DESIGN YOUR PERFECT PRICING

Back in late 2018, I hit a very low point in my career. We had a successful launch of one of the first versions of our mini webinars system, and we enrolled a bunch of clients within a span of two or three days. I think we ended up doing close to $100K in new sales with a whole bunch of clients coming on board.

We had just raised the price, and it was exciting to see a surge of cash in our bank account. I was managing the team, and I thought we were ready to handle this type of business, but I didn't do a good job of qualifying my clients. There were definitely some clients that I shouldn't have accepted into our agency, and there were some clients we just couldn't get results for.

About a month or so after we had that surge of new business, I ended up needing to refund probably 60 or 70 percent of all of those payments, which ended up being around $60K–$70K. This put me into a very deep depression, and I didn't come out of it for about a month.

I stopped interacting online. I couldn't get out of bed all day for weeks on end. I felt like I had let my team down, like I had let my family down. I had over-promised and under-delivered, which was a huge slice of humble pie.

It took about 45 days for me to get out of that depression and start rebuilding everything. The moral of the story is that, in terms of over-promising and under-delivering, you have to make sure that you do not put unnecessary stress on yourself.

Just because you CAN charge a high price point doesn't mean you SHOULD charge as high a price point as possible. Because if you ever get yourself into a situation where you realize that you can't

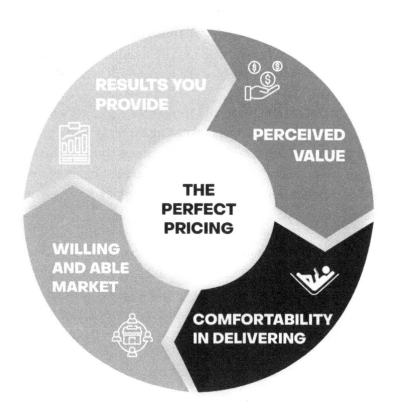

fulfill your promise, you don't want it to cripple you. And it can happen at any stage in your business.

Determining your price is an art more than a science.

The High Ticket Pricing Model melds four things together. And, if you get this right, you can avoid things like massive chargebacks and deep depression.

Here are the four elements of the model:

1. Your **perceived value** from the customer
2. Your **comfort level in being able to deliver**
3. A market that is **willing and able**
4. The **results you provide** as a result of your offer

When you combine all four of these things, you will have the perfect price that you feel comfortable charging, that people are willing to pay, and that they're able to pay because they see the results that you provide. And you don't have to worry about possibly shooting yourself in the foot and adding unnecessary stress because you charged too much.

Your Perceived Value

Perceived customer value comes down to one thing: **BELIEF.**

1. Does your customer BELIEVE that your core promise will satisfy their needs?
2. Does your customer BELIEVE in your ability to deliver?
3. Does your customer BELIEVE it's worth the price you are charging?

In order to figure out the answer to these questions, you have to ask yourself:

1. Are my promises TOO outlandish? (For example, are you promising them that they will lose ten pounds of fat in seven days?)

2. Is there any reason why my audience won't believe that I can deliver on my promise?

3. Is the price too low or too good to be true? Will people think it's a scam?

4. Is the price too high (adding unnecessary stress on my ability to deliver)?

Comfort Level in Delivery

There's nothing worse than enrolling someone you can't get results for—especially for a high-ticket item. The stress and inability to deliver will eat at you. And the last thing you want is a horde of unhappy customers demanding refunds.

Avoid unnecessary stress at all costs—it directly contradicts your High Ticket Course values. You must be comfortable in your ability to deliver within the price that you charge.

Susan, one of my group coaching students, had an offer that had been lighting the world on fire. It was a hot offer, and she knew it. We all knew it right away when she told us her calendar was already full and she was closing 60% of her calls.

People in the mentorship group started saying, "Susan, you've got to raise your price!"

But I could sense that she wasn't comfortable doing that. So I said, "Hold on. You haven't even fulfilled this offer yet. Don't raise your price. Let's dial down the ad spend and make sure that you can comfortably fulfill your promises."

Yes, a high close rate on your sales calls *might* indicate that you should raise your price. But it could also indicate that your promise might be too strong. Before you jump to raising your price, first make sure you're getting results for your customers *and* you are able to fulfill your promises.

Susan was already getting stressed out that she had so many customers. She didn't need to add a higher price to her stress.

When you get clients coming in the door, you have this immediate surge of euphoria, and then it quickly transforms into stress. Now you actually have to perform, and you have these voices in your head: *What if I don't perform? What if I can't get them results?* Those are things that you absolutely have to deal with.

Rate Your Comfort Level

Ask yourself, "If someone says yes to my offer, how confident am I in my ability to deliver?" Rate yourself on a scale of 1 to 10, 10 being super-confident, 1 being not confident at all. Then ask yourself why you chose that number.

What should happen when you get close to a 10? When you're on the phone with your perfect customer, you should be able to say with confidence, "Based on everything you've told me about your situation and what you're looking to achieve, working together is a home run, and here's why…"

When I'm talking to my ideal avatar in the agency world, that person has a list. They have customers who have already bought their products. They have a clear value proposition, and I believe their market is going to be hyper-responsive once we start to use paid ads. There's really no reason that I can see this thing failing.

There might be some risks, but I'll tell them up front that the ends justify the means. The rewards far outweigh the risks. This is a home run. And if I can't tell them that, then I'm not perfectly confident, and I have to dissect that.

Is it something in my ability to deliver? Is it my fulfillment? Is it my program? Is it my structure? I have to be able to answer that. If I'm not confident, I'll try revisiting my customer journey and focus on a promise that is more realistic.

So go back to the 1-to-10 scale. If you are rating yourself lower than a 10, maybe you're making too big of a promise. Maybe you find that once you're on the phone with these people, you realize that your claim is a little bit too outlandish, and you're not comfortable fulfilling that. When it comes to pricing, your comfort level is critical.

Your Market Must Be Both Willing *and* Able to Pay

If you're speaking to a non-motivated market, there's nothing you can do to convince them to buy your product (at scale). This is an **unwilling audience**.

Example:

Trying to sell a $1,000 DIY webinar course proved way too difficult at scale with paid ads. The vast majority of the market **did not want to learn** how to do a webinar on their own.

When I pivoted to showing *marketers and agencies* how to write million-dollar webinars for clients, demand skyrocketed.

Do you understand the difference here? Doing a slight pivot is often what some people need to do to make their offers work.

If you're speaking to an **unable** market, they won't have access to the capital to invest in your program.

Example:

Trying to sell my first course to the career development market for engineers, I was attracting unemployed engineers. They loved my content but couldn't afford $500 to learn how to level up their career. They **weren't able** to invest.

The Biggest Lesson I Learned from a Marketing Genius

Let me talk more about the last example. One of the first courses I started selling online was in the engineering career development space.

I chose to teach those interested in advancing their engineering careers by showing them exactly how I was able to get job offers, over the life of my career, from 100% of my interviews. This included significant job offers from companies like Lockheed Martin, Corning Incorporated, and other prestigious brands.

By the time I was ready to launch the course, I was pretty passionate about my topic, but I still ran into some struggles. To deal with this head-on, I hired a marketing coach and paid him $10K to help me sell this program.

He gave me some warning signs up front. He said, "There are some question marks I've got with your market and your niche selection. I'd be very nervous about this if I were you."

I replied, "Ah, don't worry about it. I'm passionate about this. I know I can help these people, so I'm going to continue forward."

Wrong answer.

The topic of my webinar was "How to Ace Your Job Interview." At the end, I pitched my career development program for $500, which taught them even more strategies for advancing their career. But I'd finish, get to the pitch to wrap up the webinar, and hear the same objection over and over again:

"Hey, I'm unemployed and I loved the training, but I really just don't have the money for it right now. Thanks for the training. See you later." Meanwhile, I was asking myself, *What is going on?*

Then I remembered the conversation that I had with my coach. He was telling me, "There's something about your market that I just don't like."

In hindsight, I could see that I was going after people who were unemployed. Naturally, they were looking to ace their job interview, even though they didn't have one lined up right at that moment, and they didn't have money to spend. While I was focused on my passion for helping people, my passion didn't turn into profits because I had an avatar who wasn't **able** to pay for my course.

What's the lesson here?

Your passions don't always turn into profits.

If you want to build a business around your passion, you have to identify something within your marketplace that people are both willing *and* able to pay for. That was my biggest lesson from my mentor, Russell Brunson.

This is wisdom to heed as you dive into discovering your market, where you have to identify who you want to serve. You have to avoid the pitfall of following your passion blindly, and instead align your passion with a market that's **willing**, has funds, and is **able** to implement what you are teaching them.

Had I known then what I know now, I would have looked at my customer journey and used a different hook to attract the right customer. Considering willing and able markets is extremely critical when developing your pricing model.

The Results You Provide

The results that you provide are the final key to this Perfect Pricing tier. Nothing justifies pricing better than prior results. And nothing allows you to feel more confident in charging what your program is worth than a laundry list of people who've crushed it.

You will always have outliers—people who get incredible, above-average results. But you should strive to raise your standard for the *average* person's results. As that level increases, your income and impact will increase. However, this should come with a very strong caveat.

A while ago, we onboarded a new client. He had been following me for a while, listening to my *Sold With Webinars* podcast, and consuming a bunch of my content. He was finally ready to work with us, so he scheduled a phone call.

On that call, he explained to me that he wanted to work with us because he saw how we had helped a previous client go from $0 to $10 million in revenue in just eight months in a similar niche to his. That was, and still is to this day, the biggest and fastest result we've gotten for a client. And my new client wanted to beat that record. It was a personal challenge of his.

At the time, I didn't think anything of that statement. I simply thought he was highly motivated, which he was. However, that should have been a red flag that I needed to readjust and set proper expectations for him.

We ended up doing very well for this client, helping him fill up his calendar with qualified sales leads and drastically improving his closing percentage with our prequalification methods. In just a few short months, his company had generated hundreds of thousands of dollars in new revenue from what we had built for him.

However, if you had seen our communication with this client over the first couple of weeks of starting this project, you'd think he was hemorrhaging money. Each email seemed like the world was on fire and that doomsday was upon us. Thankfully, our team knew how to handle it, and all was well. But this serves as a prime learning lesson: You attract exactly what you put out.

This new client simply wasn't happy with the results he was getting—even though he multiplied his initial investment many times over—because he fell short of the goal he had set for himself, which was to make more than $10 million in eight months.

If I could go back in time, I would know exactly what to say when hearing this goal. But this is why it's so important to set proper expectations for your new clients. By raising the standard of the *average* results you can get, and focusing on those average results as a measuring tool for new clients, you can help them properly set their expectations from the beginning. Because when clients get results, they won't be as happy when they use a measuring stick against an extreme success, versus measuring their outcome against the average results of the group—or even against where they first started.

Ask yourself:

- Why are people buying my program?
- Am I overpromising?
- Did I create an irresistible offer that's unrealistic to fulfill?
- Will my customers and clients get results that are at least 4–10 times their investment with me?
- What do I need to do to raise the average results in my program?

Everything that I talk about in this book is going to challenge you to provide the best offer possible to get the best results for your clients. Because if you do not put your clients front and center, I promise you, you will not last. Word is going to get out, and your program will fail.

So I am going to challenge you to do what everybody else is *not* telling you to do, and that is to raise your standards and get the best results, not in terms of your numbers, but in terms of results for your clients.

CHAPTER 7

START AT YOUR TOP TIER FOR DELIVERY AND FULFILLMENT

When it comes to delivery and fulfillment, you want to start at the top tier (the most personalized Tier 3) and work your way down. Many entrepreneurs make the mistake of starting at Tier 1 and working their way up to Tier 3, but that will quickly lead to burnout. Following the Ascension Model—instead of the Descension Model I'm teaching you—is the reason many online businesses fail.

For example, a client of mine came to me for help a couple of years ago. He was generating $120K–$150K a month with an automated webinar selling a $997 "course" (I put the word "course" in quotation marks for a reason—I'll explain shortly), but he was completely burned out.

From the outside looking in, most people would say he was crushing it. However, after seeing inside his business, it was clear to me that my client was navigating a sinking ship.

Now, if he had designed this right, his $997 one-time offer should have been on autopilot as a DIY program. Instead, he was selling this offer as lifetime access to a coaching program and promising group coaching calls seven days a week for life.

No wonder people were tripping over themselves to enroll in it!

The problems here are obvious:

1. Even though he was having consistent six-figure months, his offer wasn't scalable or sustainable.
2. His offer was *too* good. While most people sell those programs for $10K or more, my client was selling it for $997 with no other reason for the customers to purchase anything else from him. (They were already getting coaching and support with the $997 offer. Why would they pay for anything else?)
3. He needed to become an expert marketer and keep selling every single day. Otherwise, he'd go bankrupt.
4. He also had to manage a staff of 15 people just to help him service this one-time offer. Those six-figure months did nothing but suck his time dry and cause him to resent his offer.

I want to make sure you avoid burning out with "offer cannibalization." If you have a cannibalized offer that's doing $150K per month but you need a team of 15 people to support it, you hate your business, and you're forced to continually sell this course every single day just to keep your business afloat, you don't have a business model. You have a sinking ship with vanity metrics.

Descend from Tier 3 to Tier 1

Tier 3: One-On-One Coaching, Consulting, or Done-For-You

The most important reason for you to design your offer and fulfillment structure in the way I'm about to show you is because it gives clear lines of delineation for what your clients and customers get or don't get with each level. This is required to make it simple and easy to explain when you're presenting your offer to them.

It's important to start at the top tier and work your way down. Not only does working one-on-one with a premium offer get you cash-flow positive, but it also helps you to:

- Flesh out the core milestones.
- Work intimately with the clients to see how they process the content, what takes the most amount of time, and where they need help.
- Figure out if this is something you enjoy fulfilling and teaching.
- Identify the right content to teach.
- Get the best case studies for scale.

Start with one-on-one consulting (Tier 3), structured as follows:

- Bring the customer in on the core promise.
- Before each major milestone, set up a call to walk them through the next step of how to achieve the milestone. Teach them and, if possible, show them how to do it.
- At the end of the call, instruct them on what they need to do next, and schedule the next call with expectations that

they will complete the next milestone by that call, so they maintain momentum.

- In between calls, give them the ability to email you with support questions.

Your Tier 3 can also be a done-for-you service where you'd use this to validate your offer and demand first.

NOTE: If you don't have any client testimonials, you can follow my Sales Script Swipe File to start acquiring new customers. See Bonus #2 in the Bonus Section at the back of the book.

As you work closely with your clients, you can record the "teaching" sections to eliminate the one-on-one calls and structure group support calls to be more leveraged. But this is the best starting point. Let's map this out:

Let's assume that this is a 10-week program. They're going to start with their first onboarding phone call with you, and you'll say, "Here's what we're going to talk about first. Here's what I want you to do. And here's what will happen by the end." Teach them the first piece of content that's going to get them on their way to their milestone, place each step in order, and teach this to them in one-on-one calls.

In between your weekly calls, give them email support, and say, "If you have questions as you're executing the plan, shoot me an email. I'd be happy to discuss."

The client is doing homework, going through the checklist, and getting results. You have support available to them in between the calls, but you're still going to have every planned call once a week, throughout the entire length of the program.

You work one-on-one so you can get case studies, even at lower-level programs. These case studies will help you sell more.

One-on-one method benefits:

- Allows you to quickly charge a premium for your time so you can monetize and validate your core offer.
- Gives you the ability to record content for your future productized program as you deliver it.

One-on-one method pitfalls:

- Doesn't scale.
- Takes the most amount of time.

We don't need to beat a dead horse with this. Nobody wants to continue to do one-on-one if they can help it.

Tier 2: Leveraged Group Coaching

Moving on to leveraged group coaching (Tier 2):

- The entire program is released upon enrollment.
- The student follows along with the pre-recorded content and checklists.
- They receive group support in the form of open office hours, Q&A calls, and community.
- One-on-one calls with the group instructor are optional. Or, the entire program can be delivered by other trained coaches.

Visual:

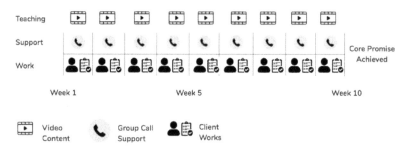

The client gets all the content released in pre-recorded videos as a standard course. They will receive support through any number of calls that you want. They have weekly group support calls or open office hours, where the expert will hold a two-hour conference call, and they can pop in if they have questions.

Or, you could have dedicated topic calls that are led by your coaches. And in between each milestone, the client is doing the work. They get the support, they get the community, and they get access to the experts. But it's much more leveraged.

Now, you're not doing one-on-one calls. You're doing group calls, and all of the teaching is completely productized. This method works to lower your fulfillment time in the program while helping more students get better results. It allows a personal touch between you and the students on a larger scale. And as it grows, you can add in more coaches to help support your fulfillment side and add more support calls, if necessary.

You create dedicated support calls for specific action items in the program. For example, you might have an "ads call," or you might have an "offer" and a "funnel" call. This can be run by one person or by a team.

Here is how our mentorship program is currently designed:

- 100-Day Implementation Program
- Core Promise: Develop a clear, simple method for creating, launching, and scaling their own high ticket course so the foundations are set up to be generating $30K–$50K per month.
- Each member is assigned a dedicated, one-on-one success coach to make sure they're on track.
- Twice-per-week support calls to assist with ads, offers, funnels, and messaging.
- Bi-weekly community coworking calls, led by me, to get work done.
- Networking community (Facebook group) to get feedback from other members as well as connect with them.

- Ticketing system available for problems not able to be handled via group and more urgent than waiting for a call.

This is how we have it set up, and it's extremely leveraged for us, while at the same time getting incredible results for our students.

> NOTE: If you'd like to learn more about our High Ticket Course and how to develop and structure your own, you can schedule a call and speak with us at: highticketcourses.com/book.

Now, you might be thinking: *OK, Joel. That program looks great. But I don't have a team in place to have that many calls. What now?*

If you're a team of just a few or even one, all you need to do is host group calls once or twice a week. Theming the calls (e.g. ads, funnels, and copy) is optional—you could simply frame these sessions as general Q&A. You are the expert. The only thing your clients care about is getting their specific questions answered.

As you start to add more clients, you can then bring on the coaches to host these Q&A calls. But, more coaches are not required to have a successful High Ticket Course.

This is important:
Your offers and programs are living, breathing, and always evolving.

Do not think that once you design it, it's going to stay static and unchanged. Your students are going to be accepting if the program evolves, and you add things or take things away. Understand that you can change it.

Every program will be slightly different depending on you, your resources, and your customers' needs.

Every market is different. Every demand is different. Every program is different. You design the rules. You are the boss of your own offers. Repeat after me:

"I am the boss of my own offers."

Tier 1: The Automated Do-It-Yourself (DIY) Program

Tier 1 is a self-paced digital program that explains your coaching and core process. Students enroll in the program and understand that there is no support community or personal coaching. It's completely do-it-yourself (DIY) and requires no additional fulfillment on the product owner. However, you will need exceptional digital marketing skills to make this work. Or, you will need to have the funds and resources to hire an exceptional digital marketing agency.

As a High Ticket Course creator, your prices should be in the thousands of dollars, which will position you to offer a DIY version to anyone who is not a good fit for your higher-tier options.

Most online course creators teach you to build this DIY version out first. The opposite is true. If you start here, you're much more likely to get overwhelmed and burn out. The HTC model has you starting with your Top Tier offer, getting clarity on that offer, and then offering a DIY model for anyone who wants your end result without the price tag of one-on-one consulting or group coaching. If you will wait until you master the top two tiers before you create this lower tier, you'll save a lot of time, energy, and money.

Why do you need to have two to three versions of your core offer? The answer is to be able to serve more of your customers. Not everyone is going to be a perfect fit for your top (most personalized and expensive) offer or want to do it all themselves without support (DIY). They still want the core promise, and you can deliver it at every level.

Decrease Time, Increase Profit

Without proper delivery and fulfillment, you will never be able to scale without spending more time in the business.

Your goal is to create delivery and fulfillment systems that help you both leverage your time *and* get better results for your customers and clients. If you want to turn your online coaching business or high ticket course into a 7-figure lifestyle, you need to answer these questions:

- What is it that your customers TRULY want?
- What is taking you the MOST time to deliver on?
- What can you cut out while your customer is still being satisfied?

As you create new offers, make sure you're providing equal value. Start with Tier 3, charge a premium price point, and make sure any new offer you create can be fulfilled and delivered faster than your comprehensive, done-for-you offerings. That's how you reduce the time spent in your business, increase your bottom line, and deliver results for your customers and clients.

CHAPTER 8

THE LAUNCH PHASE
IN 10 STEPS

Remember the Trajectory Model we talked about in Chapter 1? In Phase 1, the **Launch** phase, you're the Experimenter. This is where you're going to land on your core promise, create your Power Offer, and go from zero to at least $10K per month.

In Phase 2, you hit the **Growth** stage. Here's where you start to build the elements of the foundation and scale from $10K to $50K per month. Maybe you will bring on a team member or two to help you free up your time. This phase is about building the marketing assets to support your growth, so you can go after a larger audience and start to build this as a business model.

Then you have Phase 3, the Scale phase, where you become the leader of a growing team and go beyond $50K per month.

This book focuses heavily on Phase 1 because this is the foundation for Phases 2 and 3. If you don't launch successfully, you won't be able to sustain the growth of your business, and scaling will be impossible.

You'll need to master all 10 Steps of Phase 1 before you can move on to Phase 2.

The 10 Steps of Phase 1: Launch

Within the 10-Step roadmap to a successful launch, you will achieve three milestones: Prep, Build, and Test.

Take a look at the graphic below. Notice that your first milestone, the Prep milestone, includes Money Market, Identify Your Model, and 1-2 Sentence Power Offer. The next milestone is Build. Here you have Mini Webinar, Technical Setup, and Go Live. Your third milestone is Test, which covers Lead Generation, Applications and Phone Calls, and First Sale. Step 10 is Optimize.

Be sure to hit all three milestones. Check all the boxes in each step. Then, let that progress push you toward Growing and Scaling (Phases 2 and 3).

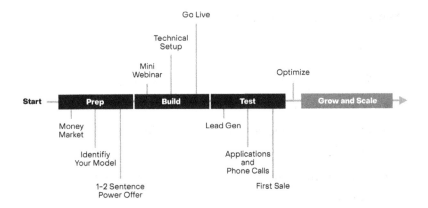

The Prep Milestone

Step 1: Your Money Market

Questions to ask yourself in this step:

- Who is my ideal client avatar?
- Who is actually willing and able to spend money with me?
- What do I *feel* they really want?
- What are their surface-level pain and desire points (my points of connection)?
- Are they already spending money?

Remember that passion doesn't always turn into profits. It's wonderful if you are passionate about something, but making sure that your passion actually connects with something that people are willing and able to spend money on is the secret to building a business that you truly love. All too often, I see people with this burning passion to help people, but they don't make that connection.

Step 2: Your Offer Model

Questions to ask yourself in this step:

- What is my model and what does it look like?
- Is my model designed to support the way I want to live?
- Does it allow me to generate cash flow *and* live my ideal lifestyle?
- Am I wanting to build a dominant business or a lifestyle business?
- Do my offers connect with each other in a seamless transition that gives my customers the best opportunity for success?

Get clear on exactly what you want to do. The biggest mistake that I see people make who are already having early success is to give away the farm. They've pigeonholed themselves into only selling that offer, and now it becomes a burden rather than a joy for them to fulfill.

Step 3: Your Power Offer

Questions to ask yourself in this step:

- Am I able to promise something that connects with a top-level desire?
- Am I able to speak to my audience in a way that both attracts people who are ready to buy now and repels my non-ideal clients?
- Does my Power Offer make them say, "YES! I want that!"?

Be aware that there are certain pitfalls that you want to avoid in this stage. For example, you don't want to attract the wrong kind of clients. You want to target a market that's willing and able to work with you. You also don't want to structure your offer in a way that demands so much of your time that you hate delivering on it. Make sure your perfect offer setup not only provides a positive experience for your ideal clients but also protects your time.

To help you create your Power Offer, see Bonus #2: Create Your Demand Faucet Power Offer toward the end of this book.

Now that you're attracting your avatar, you've created a model that supports your lifestyle, and you're making a Power Offer that gets your ideal clients to say "YES!" and buy (this is important, so don't skip it!), it's time to tackle the Build Milestone.

The Build Milestone
Step 4: Your Mini Webinar

Questions to ask yourself in this step:

- If I was forced to create a compelling message in 15 minutes or less, could I do it?
- Could I speak to my "ready to buy" avatar in a way that explains how I am different and why they should listen to me?
- Do I have a process laid out that easily explains what happens when someone works with me, so they can see the plan?
- Is my plan unique from my competitors?

Step 5: Technical Setup

We have come a long way over the last five years when it comes to the tools available to help us launch, sell, and manage our programs. I've used most of them. Right now, there is one all-in-one solution that is leading the pack in my opinion, and that's GoHighLevel (GHL).

From email marketing, funnel building, application forms, schedulers, texting, course hosting, payment processing, and phone calling, this company will save you thousands of dollars—sometimes per month. And they are incredibly affordable to use.

I've worked out a deal with them to offer you a free trial to their software at this link: highticketcourses.com/GHL

Questions to ask yourself in this step:

- How do I keep everything simple and easy to manage so I don't get bogged down in the weeds?
- Do I need to enlist assistance to get this built out for me?

Step 6: Launch Your Ads

Questions to ask yourself in this step:

- What are the key metrics that I need to monitor throughout the sales funnel?
- How do I know if my message is resonating?
- What should I be aware of when I launch my ads?

Here, you've got your Power Offer message. How do you know if people are actually clicking through and if it's actually making sense? Sure, in a perfect world, they're going to go through the entire funnel, and you're going to be making money, but we all know that shit hits the fan. So, what should you be aware of in this case?

Questions to ask yourself when shit hits the fan:

- What if people aren't responding to my Power Offer?
- How do I know if my Power Offer or mini webinar needs adjusting?
- Do I need a unique mechanism?
- Do I need to create a new mini webinar?
- Do I need to adjust my money market?

The Test Milestone

Step 7: Generating Your First Leads

Questions to ask yourself in this step:

- How do I set up the perfect opt-in page?
- How do I create a compelling headline that remains congruent with my Power Offer?

Step 8: Generating Applications and Conversations

Questions to ask yourself in this step:

- How do I analyze the applications coming through?
- How do I pre-sell the applications and pre-qualify them, so I am having simple, meaningful, and powerful enrollment conversations?

- Is my application attracting or repelling potential clients?
- What are the "buying indicators" from the applications I'm receiving, so I'm not wasting time with tire kickers?

Step 9: Closing Your First Sales

Questions to ask yourself in this step:

- How do I properly onboard these clients so they are primed for success?
- What's the first step I need to accomplish with my clients?
- Are they one-on-one? Is this a leveraged offer? What are the fulfillment requirements?

How do you make sure that your clients are getting service? You want to make sure you're providing the best experience for them while still doing this in a way that allows you to create a very lightweight and effective offer.

Blindly following the "raise your price" advice could potentially destroy your business and put you in a place that causes way more anxiety and way more stress than you need. There's a way to design this where you do not need to stress out.

Step 10: Optimizing Your System

Questions to ask yourself in this step:

- What happens if my metrics are out of KPI (Key Performance Indicators)?

- How many calls do I need to have before I know if my offer is misaligned?
- How do I know if I should raise my price? Lower my price?

The one specific area where most people fail is when they fall in love with their offer. They decide not to listen when the market says, "I do not want this offer," and they keep trying to slam a square peg into a round hole.

You need passion in this business because you want to serve your audience, but you also have to design your passion around what people want. And if people are not responding to your offer, a lead magnet will not save you.

Use the data to your advantage, and be flexible enough to pivot your Power Offer when necessary.

All these milestones occur in Phase 1, the Launch Phase. This can take people from 30 days to over 90 days to accomplish. It all depends on how fast you're able to execute, how fast you're able to get feedback on your offer, and how willing and able you are to pivot your offer.

CHAPTER 9

BUILD A PROFITABLE BUSINESS BEFORE BUILDING A BRAND

A couple of years ago, a friend of mine came to me wanting to hire my webinar agency.

I asked him what his existing assets were, and he told me he had an email list of 30,000 people. I said, "Oh, that's awesome!" because having an audience to work with is usually a good sign. It means he's probably making some decent money in his business.

I asked, "How much are you making from your list?"

He said, "Honestly, Joel, I'm making less than $1,000 a month. On a good month, I'm making probably about $800 a month from that list of 30,000 people."

I was shocked. "You've got to be kidding me! $800 a month on a good month from 30,000 people? Why do you think that is?"

He said, "Well, these people love my content, and they've been trained and have it ingrained just to read my free stuff. But they're not trained and ingrained to want to invest in any of my programs, no matter what the price point is."

Build a List of Buyers (Not Freebie Seekers)

If you've been in marketing for any length of time, you've heard this hammered over and over again: Build a list! Build a list! Build a list!

But here's the thing: A list is only valuable if it's an active and engaged list of *buyers*—not a list of freebie-seekers.

That's the big problem with building a list before you ever make an offer to them. If you train your audience to consume (not buy) your content by providing all this great free information, they're going to see you only as a great resource—like Wikipedia or Google—where information is free anytime they want. That's a recipe for disaster.

When you're building an audience—especially early on—you need to frame your messaging in a way that makes it clear that you're not doing anything for free. Your information is valuable, so you need to flip the script and attract buyers who are willing to invest in themselves.

Avoid the "Spray and Pray" Approach

Sadly, most experts are taught to grow their business using a "spray and pray" approach, but you should avoid this if you want to launch your online business.

What Is the "Spray and Pray" Approach?

- Educate!
- Give value!

- Put out lead magnets!
- Run paid ads to those lead magnets!
- Build a list!
- Go live on Facebook every day!
- Create fresh content!
- Post on social media multiple times a day!
- Share Instagram stories!
- Record YouTube videos!
- Write blog posts!
- Start a podcast!

And the list goes on and on ...

No matter how big you build an audience, you're not building an asset if they're not ready to buy. You don't want to be attracting freebie seekers with a "spray and pray" approach.

Now, don't get me wrong. These are all valuable activities, but only when they're done at the right time and in the right order.

First Things First: Lead With Your Offer, Not With Your Brand

Even if you're making over $100K per month, keep in mind that everything should be done in the correct order. Everything listed above is a low-level activity that supports your vanity metrics (e.g., likes, shares, and followers). But these don't necessarily move the needle.

The book that hit the nail on the head for me is the same book I mentioned in the introduction: *How to Create Irresistible Offers*[3] by Bob Bly. In this book, Bly takes this concept of going after the right market at the right time with the right message, and he puts a dollar value on it.

PERFORMANCE DEGRADATION AS BRAND CONTENT INCREASES AND OFFER CONTENT DECREASES			
Copy Platform	**Brand Content**	**Offer Content**	**Approximate Cost Per Sale**
Primarily Offer-Driven	10%	90%	$50-$100
Offer Leads - Brand Follows	25%	75%	$200-$250
Brand Leads - Offer Follows	75%	25%	$400-$600
Primarily Brand-Driven	90%	10%	$800-$1,000

This is what his chart is saying: As you create content, the structure of the content and its message will directly correlate with your cost per sale.

There are two types of content: brand-driven content and offer-driven content. Brand-driven content—also known as educational content—is going to be all of the messages that really have no call to action. And your offer-driven content is going to be, "I want to help you do X, Y, and Z. Here's what to do next."

If you have a platform that is primarily offer-driven, 90% of that message is created around an offer and just 10% of it is created

---

[3] Robert W. Bly, *How to Create Irresistible Offers: The Easiest Way on Earth to Make Your Marketing Generate More Leads, Orders, and Sales* (Delray Beach, FL: American Writers & Artists, 2009), p. 3.

around your brand. Your approximate cost per sale is going to be $50-$100. (These are all just relative numbers that Bob Bly chose to illustrate his point. This is not saying you're going to acquire customers for this amount. He's just saying that this is going to be your lowest cost per sale.)

As you reduce your offer content and increase your brand content, your cost per sale will go up by two to four times each iteration. By the bottom of the chart, you have primarily brand-driven (educational) content. Your cost per sale is going to be extremely high because it's not offer-based, direct response marketing.

In the introduction, I talked about one particularly sleepless night when I picked up this book and changed the course of my business and my life. Seeing this chart was really the lightbulb moment for me: *What the hell am I doing? I need customers right now. Why am I trying to build these long-form content machines when I would be willing to bet that I've got customers who are willing to cut a check for me right now if I present a compelling offer?* The game changed for me here.

Ask yourself:

- If someone is looking to buy NOW, what are they most interested in?
- What do they already know about the problem?
- What do they already know about a potential solution? Have they tried to solve this?
- What is bugging them?
- What have they already looked for?
- What have they tried and failed?

Go back to the "closest to the conversion hole" analogy. Focus on the 3–10% of your audience that has tried and failed because it will get your mind thinking about exactly what you need to be saying to those people.

Your message should be speaking directly to their problems, getting them to say, "Yes, I'm interested in buying right now."

Big Money from Small Lists

To further the point of not needing a large list to make good money, we'll go back to my client I've referenced earlier —Brad.

Brad had been running his Power Offer and mini webinar to attract clients for a few months. But after one of our consulting calls, he knew that he was leaving money on the table with some of the leads he spoke to but hadn't yet enrolled. So, he decided to host an informal, virtual event called "Beers with Brad."

He invited the small list that he had curated to this webinar. He didn't know who would show or how many. His only goal was to show whoever attended the recent results he had been getting from his trading system.

When "Beers with Brad" started, five people showed up. By the end of the informal, non-scripted call, four out of the five attendees enrolled in his $3,000 program, for a total of $12K in new revenue.

Why did this work? Simply put, these people were already primed with an offer the first time they were exposed to Brad. They weren't expecting free education. They knew Brad had a program. They just needed the right time to join.

Avoid Content Marketing for Vanity Metrics

There's nothing wrong with content marketing, but only if it's done at the right time and in the right order. When you do content marketing in Phase 1, you are only getting vanity metrics. You end up cannibalizing your own content. And worst of all? You train your audience to get only free material from you.

In Phase 1, you should only focus on your conversion content, which is the Minimum Viable Funnel (MVF). Your MVF ensures that once prospects are within your grasp, they will convert.

But in Phases 2 and 3, content marketing is key. Your content acts like a magnetic charge, repelling or attracting your pool of prospects. Your content marketing is designed to maintain and attract those who are still interested in buying—just not right now.

CHAPTER 10

SCALE YOUR HIGH TICKET COURSE BUSINESS

Two or three years ago, I thought I was ready to scale my agency. I thought we were in growth mode, and I was convinced that I needed to invest in systems, processes, and procedures. So, for six months I tried doing it on my own, and it absolutely melted my brain. I hated every moment of it.

After I went to a mastermind event in Las Vegas, I decided I was going to hire a COO because it seemed like the right thing to do. I was the CEO, and I had heard that I needed to hire a COO because they had the skills that I lacked.

I hired a fractional COO and paid them $80 an hour for 30 to 35 hours a week to build out processes and procedures, and to manage the company. Now, I had a smokescreen of lead flow. It wasn't consistent, but one month I got a surge of clients, then the next month it was a trickle, and then I got another surge the month after that. It was an unrealistic view of what my business was actually doing. There's a very clear difference—just because I had cash in the bank didn't mean that I was ready to scale and invest in my team.

I worked with the COO for four or five months, and I realized in the end that I didn't want a big team. We had invested in Infusionsoft, we had hired other experts to help us build the right systems, processes, and procedures, and I was building something that I didn't want. Ultimately, I realized I didn't really want a big agency.

Grow and Scale in Phases 2 & 3

Growing, scaling, and adding in content marketing takes time and effort. It's important to get this in the right order if you want to semi-retire instead of suffer from burnout.

In this chapter, we'll cover what you need for Phases 2 and 3, which is how to grow and scale everything you built in Phase 1.

Now is the time to begin priming yourself with the following questions:

- When do I implement marketing and branding into my funnel?
- How do I create magnetic content?
- Do I create a group?
- What do I do for email marketing?
- What are my stories to include in my content package?
- Who do I hire first? How much do I pay them?
- What are my expectations when hiring team members?

These are all the things that will happen as you start to grow and scale into your leadership role, and they should happen in the right order.

Things will happen that may pull your attention away from the main focus, but the good news is that you've got an offer that converts.

Think Before You Grow

It's important to ask yourself what you want from your business. Not everyone wants the same things. Some are content with five-figure months while others want to scale to six figures and beyond.

Ask yourself:

What do I really want my business to provide for me?

- Is this going to be a cash cow?
- Am I an entrepreneur who's interested in growth?

It's totally fine if you're interested in accomplishing other things, but you have to get clear on what you really want your business to do for you.

What do I feel about team building?

- If I had to manage 10 contractors/employees, would I be happy?
- If I had to manage 2–3 contractors/employees, would I be happier?

I like going on the ends of the extremes (even though 10 contractors and employees is not really extreme). For those of you who are just entering this new venture, you are going to need to get help as you continue to grow, unless you want to stay small.

How comfortable am I with investing in my business?

- Do I hold on too tight to my finances?
- Do I understand that things like advertising are investments into my business to get back my time? Or do I view them as expenses?

These simple questions will start to prepare you for if, when, and how you're ready to grow this business.

Planning a 7-Figure Run Rate: How the Tiers and Trajectory Work Together

This is not fluff that I made up. This is backed by experience, and I've coached other people through this growth plan. You can determine the level at which you want to play, even up to 7 figures.

Getting to a 7-figure run rate is really simple with the right plan. It's roughly $85K per month, and that's it. If you've never hit $85K per month, and it seems like a stretch—that's totally fine. But I promise you, when you start hitting those milestones of $10K a month, then $30K a month, then $60K, $70K, and $85K a month, it's not so difficult once you've successfully moved through the three phases. That could be 10 clients at an $8,500 average order value, or that could be 20 clients at an average order value of $4,250.

Let's determine what it takes to actually make that happen. Because those are not difficult milestones to achieve when you understand what it takes to get there.

As we discussed earlier, we have two core models that make up our execution plan. We have the Trajectory, which are the phases in which we grow. This includes the Launch Phase, the Growth Phase, and the Scale Phase, as well as the three different types of people that you need to become as you develop through those phases.

Then we have your High Ticket Course model, where you have two or three tiers of your signature offer. They meld together. We're going to walk through the three phases now, so you can see exactly how to apply the High Ticket Course model to the Trajectory plan.

THE HIGH TICKET COURSES DESCENSION MODEL

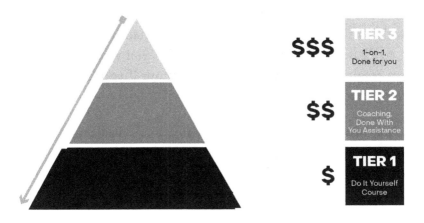

Example:

Let's say you're just getting started and you are launching a new offer. You start off in Phase 1 of the Trajectory by only launching your Tier 3 course, the most premium level. That's either one-on-one, done-for-you, or whatever is the most intimate level offering.

In this example, you will start out with a $3,500 offer, and your goal here will be $10K per month. You will want to reach that goal as fast as possible. So, at $3,500 you will really only need three clients to get to that $10K per month mark. If you have a 30% closing ratio of people who you get on the phone, then you will only need to have 11 conversations to get those three clients.

You will follow an advertising model. You will use ads to save your time and get your message out there as fast as possible. Your benchmarks will be a bare minimum return on investment of at least 4X. In this specific example, a 4X return on investment will be a cost per sale of about $700.

Eleven conversations will turn into three clients, getting you to that $10K per month mark. After one to two months of successfully doing this, you will have validated your offer and now you will be ready to take the next step. As you transition from Phase 1 to Phase 2, you will validate your offer, you will get great client results, and you will start to figure out if you like working in this niche.

If the answer is yes, and if you're getting those clients results, you will introduce a Tier 2, leveraged offer in addition to your Tier 3. (Remember, when you start out with Tier 3, you don't necessarily have any content created. This is all going to be a one-on-one consulting session, where you work with people to get results.)

So you now have two offers. You will bump your Tier 3 offer to $6,500 and will introduce Tier 2 at the same price where Tier 3 was initially: $3,500. At this point, it will be okay to raise your price because you know you have a successful offer that you are confident you can fulfill. So if you average those two together, the average offer price will be $5,000.

Your goal here in Phase 2 will be roughly $30K–$50K per month. This means that you will need six clients to hit that goal if you assume a 30% closing ratio, which is typical.

After consistently achieving your goal of $30K–$50K per month, you will arrive at another fork in the road: transitioning from Phase 2 to Phase 3.

Some people will say, "This is awesome. I've never had this much freedom. I've never had this much money in the bank. I've never had this much profit in my business. I just want to maintain this." And that is totally fine. Any further growth will cause some people to hit a time barrier.

Twenty conversations a month is probably about four to five sales conversations per week. And then there's the fulfillment side. If they're doing this as a one-man-band, they're going to be tapped out relatively quickly because there's not much more they can—or want—to do.

I often see people float around between this $30–$50K per month mark as a one-man band, or maybe with an assistant, to help them help free up some time.

As you come to this fork in the road, you will have that decision that you need to make. Do you want to grow this even bigger? Or do you want to just maintain and enjoy what you've built?

If you choose to move into Phase 3, you will start building out your team. Maybe you will hire an enrollment specialist to make those sales calls. Instantly, you will be relieved of 20 conversations a week, and that's a huge weight lifted off your shoulders. Maybe you will hire a coach to help with fulfillment. Either way, these are the things that you need to focus on to start freeing your time.

Here in Phase 3, you will either phase your one-on-one (Tier 3) program out completely or will drastically raise the price because that's not your focus anymore. The main purpose of a Tier 3 program is just to get cash coming in the door (something you will no longer need to do in Phases 2 and 3 of the Trajectory).

If you want to continue to work with people one-on-one, that's fine, but let's assume you are going to phase out Tier 3 for this example. So you will raise your Tier 3 now to $12K. You will raise your Tier 2 (group coaching program) to $6,000 after you've had a few months of clients getting great success, and you can justify a higher price point. You will implement Tier 1—which is a Do-It-Yourself Model—for $2,000. Your average offer price here now is $6,500.

Let's look at the math as you become the leader who is building that small but mighty team in Phase 3.

Your goal here will be to hit $85K per month and beyond. You'll need to have 13 clients every single month on a front-end rate. You'll need to have 44 conversations. Assuming a cost per sale of $700, that's going to give you an ROI of 9.75X.

These are not falsely claimed numbers. These are numbers that I have seen our students hit. What I'm doing here is giving you a roadmap. And if you have an offer that people want, if you get leads coming in, and if you close 25–30% of these conversations, this is what can happen.

Some Key Items to Note for Transparency:

What we're talking about here is only relying on advertising, with no internal marketing to your list that you're generating. Your list is one of your greatest assets, but that's excluded from this book.

Also not included are back-end sales—offers made to your existing customers. That's another topic outside of this discussion but something you should not ignore.

You will deal with fluctuating ad costs. That's the name of the game. The bare minimum ROI that you should shoot for is 4X return on ads. That gives you that cushion that you need so you can say, "This is comfortable. I can add cost fluctuations and survive the testing period that I need to do." Many times you'll earn higher than a 4X return on ad spend, but this gives you plenty of margin to work with.

Define Your Goal

Take a moment to evaluate your income goal. Would you be happy with consistent $10K months? Or $30K months, running your business by yourself with one or two subcontractors? Maybe it's $85K and beyond. Ask yourself what you really want. There is no wrong answer here.

No matter your goal, I'm not here to cast judgment, but I do want to challenge you a bit. When I first started out, I was struggling to make consistent $10K–$20K months. If someone told me back then that I would eventually be running a successful multi 7-figure digital agency and coaching business, believing them would have been a stretch.

Figure out how much you need to make per month to not only cover all of your expenses but also give, save, and invest. What will it take for you to live a truly free and happy life?

Define your goal number and then ask yourself: *What is the first monetary milestone that I need to hit?* Set monetary micro milestones so you can validate that you're on the right track.

A word of caution, though: As you stretch toward your goal, you're probably going to get some resistance. Again and again, I've seen limiting beliefs sabotage perfectly good intentions. That's why it's so important to define your "why." What you're doing is never as important as why you're doing it.

As you read the next section, take some time to define your why. Then, work through the "Perfect Day" exercise. After that, we'll tackle the "Lack Mentality Mindset" in Chapter 11.

Define Your Why

Recently, I discovered a HISTORY Channel series called *The Selection: Special Operations Experiment*, where civilians went through Special Operations Forces training for 10 days.

Approximately 50 people started the journey, but only three people finished. They were taken through rigorous exercises, and at the end of the event, there were only four people remaining. The last thing that they had to do in the training program was called "The Long Walk," and that's exactly what it was.

They were sent on an undetermined, undefined walk with a 50- or 60-pound rucksack on their back—up a mountain. Some of the hills were like vertical inclines that they had to climb up. They had to just keep walking until they hit five checkpoints.

They had no idea how long the course was. They had no idea what time they had to meet. They just had to go on this Long Walk until it ended.

This was one of the most impactful things that I have ever observed from both a mentality and a commitment standpoint because, in the end, four people started The Long Walk, but one dropped out and only three people finished. Even after making it through the ten days, that one person couldn't finish and ended up dropping out at the end.

All of the training leaders met the final three people at the top of the hill and said, "Congratulations, you're done with the training. What was the one 'why' that got you up the hill?"

I could see how extremely powerful this was because their one "why" is what kept them moving forward when they faced adversity. These people got beaten. They got destroyed over the course of 10 days. Civilians—not military personnel. But they wanted to test their mentality and their wherewithal to figure out if they had what it took to go through Special Operations Forces training.

And that question—what is your "why"—was asked not only at the top of the hill but throughout the entire ten days. *What is your "why?" Why are you here?*

If they gave an answer that was surface level, like, "Oh, I want prove to myself that I can do this," they would get asked again: *No, tell me why you are here.* And the people who couldn't figure out a clear "why" all dropped out. For the rest, when the going got tough, that "why" was what kept them pushing forward.

The Perfect Day Exercise

Even though it may not be an easy task, I want you to discover your "why."

What helped me define my "why" was to design my perfect day. And I want to challenge you to design your perfect day because it could lead you down the right path to define your core "why."

So ask yourself some questions (there is no wrong answer):

- How many days per week do you want to work?
- What time do you wake up?
- What time do you go to bed?
- What are your working hours?
- When do you exercise?
- When is family time?
- When do you schedule personal time for yourself?
- How much money do you want?

Take the time now to write down the answers to these questions and any others you can think of. Your answers are going to help you start to really define what it is that you want to get out of your business and out of your life.

When I first started my journey, I was chasing the money. And when you chase the money, you can go down a lost, misled path. Now, that's not to say that you don't need money to survive, but I kept chasing a never-ending goal: I wanted to have a multi-7-figure agency so I could stand up on stage and get all these great awards.

Everything I wanted was focused on money, but any time I made more money, I never felt better. It didn't really satisfy me. It didn't really give me the core drivers that I was looking for.

About a year-and-a-half ago, I was sitting with my wife and I said, "You know what, Maryjo, I'm going to take Fridays off now. I'm just going to do it." I didn't plan for it. I didn't know if I could even do it. But our son was born, and our daughter was on the way. We had certain things that we wanted to do with our son before our daughter arrived. So that next week, we took Friday off and we went to the African Lion Safari in Toronto. It was fantastic!

From that point on, I've never worked a Friday. The business now takes a backseat to my life, and that's what happened when I defined my perfect day. My "why" became clear: I want to put my family and my lifestyle first—above the business.

Success in business comes down to three things:

- Knowing exactly what you want
- Following a map that shows you how to get it
- Showing up consistently, every day

Defining your perfect day is an exercise that will help you find *your* ideal life.

CHAPTER 11

CHALLENGE YOUR LIMITATIONS

*"I've realized that instead of following the trends,
what you want to do is you want to identify the trends,
but not follow them."*

—Steve Aoki, in *Tools of Titans* (by Tim Ferriss)

When I read this quote, it hit me personally, as I'd say I'm rather self-aware, and I'm always taking an external viewpoint as to what is going on in my life and my surroundings, trying to figure out what works and what doesn't.

More specifically, what hit me was to *identify the trends but not follow them.*

This really solidified my stance to be the man on a mountaintop looking down on the town, just observing what's going on. It's critical to choose the right path before setting out on the path—whether it's choosing the right diet, choosing the right mentor, choosing the right course, or choosing the right system and the right methodology—to make millions.

Frequently, when trying to figure out which path to take, it seems like the loudest noise in the marketplace steals and keeps our attention because it's making so much noise that we want to follow, even though that might not be the best path for us.

Are you able to take a step back and objectively identify the trends? Is the trend to follow that loud person, that loud mentor, that loud guru, or that loud whatever-it-is? Is that truly the right path for you, or are they just making a lot of noise in the marketplace to attract and mesmerize you?

I took this quote to heart, and it really helped shape my thinking to figure out how to best serve my audience. And, ultimately, how to show you the best path to living a semi-retired lifestyle, with a low-stress, high-impact, expert-based business as a course marketer.

How You Think Is Everything

We are bound by the way we think. If we have doubts and invisible limits in our minds, we need to learn how to expand our limits. Growth happens at the outset of trying new things and pushing our comfort zone. How we think about everything is a mindset that shapes our lives, every single day.

When I first got started in digital marketing, I was exposed to experts like Frank Kern and Jeff Walker, and their ability to create million-dollar launches in a day.

However, the first infopreneur, as far as I know, to do a million dollars in a single day was John Reese. There seemed to be a lot of bravado and bragging about doing a million dollars in a day, and it became a gold standard.

We need mental breakthroughs from a limiting belief to make us feel like something is really possible. For example, running a four-minute mile was not "possible" until Roger Bannister broke this supposed human barrier. Within a short time, many others were running four-minute miles.

While I didn't really have a burning desire to do a million-dollar launch in a day, it gave me confidence for my vision and mission. I thought, *Wow, if they're doing a million in a day, imagine what's possible if I do this expert-based business over six months, or a year, or however long it takes.* It stuck in my mind because it showed me what was possible.

A new kind of "four-minute mile" happened in November 2017. In my mind, it became a milestone to achieve. I had been holding the concept of a million dollars in a day for about four years as my invisible goal, but I never heard of anybody else really breaking it in any industry.

Then, all of a sudden, I saw an article from *Business Insider,* reporting: "Amazon seizes half of all online Black Friday sales in an 'eye-popping' show of dominance."[4] (Dennis Green, November 24, 2017).

They did a billion dollars in revenue in 24 hours!

As mentioned above, not long ago, digital marketers were bragging about doing a mere million dollars in 24 hours. Amazon beat

---

[4] Dennis Green, "Amazon Seizes Half of All Online Black Friday Sales in an 'Eye-Popping' Show of Dominance," Business Insider, *Business Insider*, November 24, 2017, https://www.insider.com/amazon-takes-half-of-all-online-black-friday-sales-so-far-2017-11.

Joel Erway

November 27 at 4:08pm · Lewiston · 🌐 ▾

Not long ago, Internet Marketers were bragging about making $1MM in 24 hours.

Amazon beats that by 1,000x on Friday and claimed 50% of all online US retail sales.

What's next?

Amazon seizes half of all online Black Friday sales in an 'eye-popping' show of dominance

A new report by CBH Insights shows that Amazon has dominated Black Fridays so far.

BUSINESSINSIDER.COM

that by a thousandfold on Black Friday while also claiming 50% of all online U.S. retail sales. Holy crap!

Wow. Now, I had a new goal. A million dollars in a day was possible, and now so was a billion dollars.

What Amazon did blew my mind with the possibilities for digital marketing and online businesses.

But wait. Let me ask you a question: How long do you think I held on to this limiting belief of a billion dollars in 24 hours? Remember, it took four years to break the record of a million dollars, but a billion in 24 hours? How long do you think that record lasted?

Well, my client and friend Wilco de Kreij, who runs a couple of software companies, UpViral and Connectio, sent me a note that read: "Hey Joel, check this out. Alibaba."

Wilco De Kreij Joel Erway
https://www.nytimes.com/.../busi.../alibaba-singles-day.html

Alibaba's Singles Day Sales Hit New Record of $25.3 Billion

The shopping extravaganza — China's version...

NYTIMES.COM

Like · Reply · Remove Preview · 🌟 1 · November 27 at 4:18pm

Alibaba's single-day sales hit a new record of $25.3 billion. The previous record of a billion in 24 hours was surpassed by 25-fold.[5]

Expand Your Limits and Goals

I tell you all this because I want you to think about what's really possible for your business. When I talk about High Ticket Courses and mention clients going from $0 to $10 million in less than six months, or $0 to $1.2 million in two-and-a-half months, my prospects can't even comprehend it. Again, I'm not trying to pressure you to duplicate these stats. That's not my ultimate goal.

---

[5] Tiffany Hsu, "Alibaba's Singles Day Sales Hit New Record of $25.3 Billion," The New York Times (*The New York Times*, November 11, 2017), https://www.nytimes.com/2017/11/10/business/alibaba-singles-day.html.

When I make what appear to be lofty claims like $85K per month, I want you to look within and evaluate your thoughts and mind-sets for limiting beliefs.

How does your brain respond if you ask: *What's a goal I've never dreamed of before? What do I currently believe is impossible?*

The borders of my own limiting beliefs kept shifting. They went from a thousand dollars in a day, to a million dollars in a day, to a billion dollars in a day, to a staggering $25 billion in a single day.

I'll say it again: *How you think is everything.* It's time to expand the limits of your mind and understand that what you think is impossible is likely quite possible. Start expanding your thinking.

Think bigger!

What's Possible with Power Offers and Mini Webinars

Occasionally, I'll have clients who come to me with ideas that they want to launch, and they'll hit record numbers in record time. For example, one of my clients wanted help developing an offer for a done-for-you Amazon service. In essence, he would build automated Amazon stores for clients, charge them $30K, and in return, he would help them quickly get to $100K per month in revenue with their stores.

Now, it was a great offer, and we helped him scale very, very quickly. In fact, to my knowledge, I believe that he is the fastest person in the ClickFunnels community to grow to $10 million. We were able to help him go from zero to $10 million in five months with just a very simple Power Offer and mini webinar funnel. I think he did his first million in less than 30 days. Now, that's not typical, but it did happen.

We do have other clients with similar stories ...

One of my first clients was Nathan. Nathan had an idea for a course that he wanted to sell. He would help people with viral contest marketing. I brought him on as a one-on-one consulting client. We set up this exact same system that I talked about in this book. Nathan went from zero to $13K in just two weeks, and then he scaled that up to about $70K per month shortly after that.

Roger, an energy consultant, had a course that taught other people how to make money by going to business owners and showing them a no-cost solution for saving money on their energy bills. He had struggled for years in the digital marketing space, trying to figure out how to sell this course.

After he approached me, I realized he had a great opportunity. So we worked together, and within a couple of weeks, we were able to launch his system. He closed his first $5,000 and $7,000 programs shortly after that. He's since gone on to six-figure months, and he's now completely productized with multiple versions of his course, and he's doing very, very well.

Another client of mine wanted to teach people how to build a successful cabinet startup business. Within the first day of launching his program, he generated his first lead for under a dollar, and he generated his first ten applications for less than 50 bucks total. That very first lead that came into his system he was able to close for $10K. He has since gone on to grow and scale that program.

Then, there's Nicholas, who's in the health and fitness space, working directly with clients to hit their fitness goals. After following my advice with Power Offers, he was able to generate 153 calls for $3.68 each (not typical). As a result, he generated $28,898 in revenue from just $241.80 in ads.

Karwanna helps business owners land government contracts. Before joining High Ticket Courses, she had tried plenty of other marketing strategies. What she learned was that she really needed a Power Offer to get the right people in the door, fast. Within just a couple of months, she quickly scaled her offer to $100K. Now, she has an endless demand for her offer. She has moved into a new office and is expanding her business.

Earlier, I mentioned one of our most impressive client success stories. We helped him go from zero to $400K per month in just six months using a mini webinar funnel.

Most of these clients never dreamed these numbers were possible until they started hitting them. The realm of possibility with High Ticket Courses is beyond what most people imagine.

Abundance Versus Scarcity

Garrett Gunderson has a great book based on financial myths called *Killing Sacred Cows: Overcoming the Financial Myths that are Destroying Your Prosperity*. The first myth he busts is the "myth of a finite pie." He's essentially saying there are a lot of people who think there's a finite resource of "pie."

The pie is what we cut up for us all to share; the more we have, the less others have, and vice-versa. The myth is that the more we take, the more we own, then the more we're taking away from somebody else.

How does this relate to us as High Ticket Course experts?

Well, in the expert-based space, you'd think we wouldn't have a scarcity mindset because we're simply trying to teach others a skill set. We're trying to teach them new ideas, or increase their knowledge, or show them how to better themselves using the techniques, strategies, and methodologies we've developed. It seems logical and rational that we can't use up brainpower.

But when we incorporate the business element for expert course creators, our mindset quickly goes from an abundance mindset to a scarcity mindset. Suddenly, we now think that because we're charging money, we need to worry about competitors grabbing market share and others stealing our intellectual property, using it to launch their own business.

Of course, that may or may not happen.

We have to attack scarcity at the root cause because I want you—as an expert, as a course creator, whose mission it is to help other people expand—to maintain the mindset of abundance when you're building your business.

Because if you start to operate your business from scarcity, you might say, "I don't want to give away all my stuff because I feel like I'm just going to be creating my competitors," or, "I want to withhold some things because I don't want everyone to know the real secret sauce." This type of thinking really does happen, and if you go into business with this mindset, it won't serve you and will suppress your growth and income.

Garrett points to the idea of the finite pie, where once you take a piece of the pie, there's much less of the total pie left. But that's really not the case—especially when sharing your expertise. To be quite honest, some of the best offers and some of the best programs that I've seen in terms of financial success and impact have been when we are teaching others exactly how to do what we're doing, holding nothing back.

As an example, one of my clients, Steven, teaches how to launch a seven-figure cabinet startup company because that's exactly what he did himself. He launched *his* seven-figure cabinet startup company in Orlando, Florida, and he wanted to show others how to do it for their business.

Steven launched his course, and from the very first email opt-in, he closed a deal for $10K. He has since scaled that to multiple-five-figures per month, and he's on his way to building his own High Ticket Course business. His phenomenal success was a result of thinking in terms of abundance and not scarcity.

Now, alternatively, he could have thought, *I don't want to give away all my secrets because I could be training my competitors, and that's the wrong way to go.* But in reality, once you start teaching other people what you are doing, you're not necessarily giving them a slice of *your pie*.

You're not sharing your pie or even a *piece* of your pie. **You're creating more pies.** You're creating more opportunities that come from having more influencers and having more people in the space who are now servicing and developing your market as a whole.

One of the courses I launched taught people how to run successful marketing and sales webinars. I wanted to test the idea that our marketing message, in general, showed other experts how to create webinars on their own.

While we were having some success, it wasn't lighting the world on fire—that is, until I did the JV promotion with Kevin Rogers that I mentioned in Chapter 2. Even though Kevin is a well-known copywriter, he trains other copywriters to help them get their own copywriting clients and build their business. He holds nothing back. He shares everything revolving around writing copy, reviewing copy, and even teaching copy, too. He's an excellent guy—*a giver*.

Our joint venture webinar crushed it. It was the best promotion we'd ever done. I'd estimate we did around $30K in sales from that promotion. When I told my ads manager about it, he said, "Well, why don't we try another angle and teach people how to build *their own webinar agency?*" Inspired, we created new ads and new hooks to promote this message, teaching the exact same thing, but going after a different market by showing them how to do what I did to build the agency.

Our cost per lead dropped by 60 or 70 percent, indicating that the demand was extremely high. I had to change my thinking for this promotion because at first, I was afraid I'd be training other people to run webinar agencies, and I'd be competing with them to get clients.

But in reality, if I'm training other people how to write million-dollar webinars, I'm helping the entire market, and I am creating more pies and more opportunities for everybody in my niche. Even if I was training some of my competitors, each person or agency is going to express their own unique style and preferences to attract clients.

A prospect might relate more to me or someone else, even though we're promising the same result and offering a similar service. When we're hired to create a webinar for somebody, it's because they like my style or my story a little bit better. Prospective clients are either going to resonate more with me or with another service provider.

Thinking from scarcity and worrying about training your competitors is the wrong approach. Have a mindset of abundance to stimulate more opportunity in the marketplace.

If you have a unique methodology, then you can teach other entrepreneurs how to use your system to go out and service their own client base. If I've not been clear enough yet, my advice for you is: Don't withhold information. Go for it with an abundance mindset and not from scarcity. You'll create far more opportunities in your life when you don't withhold the keys to the kingdom and when you're totally open and willing to share all of your knowledge with all types of customers.

If you come from a mindset of abundance, you'll create far more opportunities than you could ever imagine. Don't withhold all of your secrets.

CHAPTER 12

WHAT IS YOUR GREATEST ASSET?

"The rich don't work for money, they work for assets which make money FOR them."

— **Robert Kiyosaki**

Assets are, in any other market and lots of other niches, things that produce revenue and a compounding return on revenue. As an information marketer who sells your intellectual property, you have incredible assets that require very little to produce, unlike real estate where you have to actually purchase land, a house, a condominium, or a commercial property.

Your most valuable assets come from the intellectual property you have in your mind. I want you to think about how you develop your intellectual property.

What are the core assets you need to be successful in your business? Think about how you can build your assets in a way that won't take away tons of your time because, remember, your whole goal is to live a semi-retired lifestyle. You don't want to be a slave to your business. You want the business to work for you.

You want your efforts to produce compounding returns from your intellectual property assets. Any content you create, for example, becomes an asset. Think about the different types of assets you can create, accumulate, and appreciate over time.

I learned about this concept from one of my mentors, Travis Sago, and want to recognize him for it. Travis had this great story to illustrate how you can view your own intellectual property as assets.

Travis said, "Robert Kiyosaki, from *Rich Dad, Poor Dad*, collected $45 million in royalty payments between 2007 and 2010, when real estate was tanking and investors were literally losing their own homes. This was not rent from his real estate property, but royalties from his intellectual property."

Intellectual property is the ultimate asset for someone who wants to retire or semi-retire 20 or 30 years sooner without debt. Debt will bankrupt a person when things go wrong—and things go wrong often—but intellectual property does not have the same issues as real estate.

You see, you create your intellectual property once, and then you can rent it, sell it, and license it to collect those royalties for years, without ever depleting it or having it depreciate.

In fact, intellectual property is one of the only assets which becomes more valuable the more you use it.

Your IP Is Your Ticket to HTC

How does Brian, a client of mine, sell $5,000 and $20K hand-stand courses to the tune of over $3 million? Mind you, he's doing this successfully in a handstand niche where his competitors are selling $10 courses or producing free content on YouTube.

His secret? He never *ever* sells handstands.

He's not selling what he's *doing*. He sells to the *aspiration* of who his audience will become once they're able to do a handstand.

Do you think his marketing message is: "I want to show you how to do a handstand. If I offer to show you how to do a handstand, would you take me up on that offer?"

No, that's not what he's doing.

He's doing what I call aspirational marketing and identity value creation. He's speaking to their aspirations—who they want to become—and creating a new identity for them which, in essence, is creating higher internal perceived value for his offer.

Brian is helping them become a brand new person because doing a handstand is not as simple as one step. There are lots of steps they need to be able to do before they can achieve the handstand.

Once they are able to do that handstand, they're at the pinnacle of their health. It represents them being in the best shape of their life. It represents them being in the greatest health of their life.

He's not selling handstands. He's selling aspirations. That's why he's able to get people to commit up to $20K to hang out with him and learn more about how he can help them live their best lives.

Once you develop your intellectual property (IP) and package it in different ways into sellable assets, you will create your own "virtual money machine" (like Brian) and become the High Ticket Course Expert of your niche.

Remember, High Ticket Course Experts transform their IP into a lucrative business model that provides them with the lifestyle freedom they desire. Leveraging your expertise is how you attain semi-retirement.

The rich don't work for money; they collect rent, dividends, and royalties from their assets. Your intellectual property is an asset. You don't have to sell cheap shit to the masses when you can sell valuable assets to the classes.

I don't know about you, but I don't want to wait until I'm 63 years old to save up $5 million, so I can pull out 4% a year (which is what many wealthy people do, even though $200K a year isn't bad). I want to semi-retire NOW and enjoy my family. That's why I've not only worked to become a High Ticket Course Expert but I also wrote the book on it so you could take what I've learned, apply it, and become a semi-retired High Ticket Course Expert, too.

AFTERWORD

March 20, 2019

My phone buzzed in my pocket.

We were finishing up our final day of a two-day mastermind with my private clients down in St. Augustine Beach, Florida. They had all paid between four and five figures just to be there, sharing wisdom with each other, so my focus was on my clients. I hadn't had a chance all day to check my messages.

When the private mastermind event ended, I finally picked up my phone and saw a message from one of my old fraternity brothers, Chris.

Now, it was weird to get a message from Chris because I hadn't seen him in at least five years. So his message definitely got my attention.

I opened up the message and found a picture—a picture of my company logo, The Webinar Agency, on a hotel seminar room sign.

Because I was hosting this event in a small hotel in St. Augustine Beach, for him to be able to take a picture of the same sign hanging up in the hallway, just outside the door, surprised the heck out of me.

Chris Rumpler · 1st
Network Deployment Engineering at Synoptek

MAR 20, 2019

 Chris Rumpler · 4:56 PM
Joelllll

 Joel Erway · 5:25 PM
Wtf

Along with the picture, he asked, "Are you here? Is this you?"

I laughed and texted back, "Yeah, why?"

He wrote, "Well, about 20 of us are here for CJ's wedding."

"You gotta be kidding me," I said. Then, I walked outside to see a
whole group of my fraternity brothers who I've not seen in almost

10 years. We hugged, and I asked, "What's going on? Why are you guys here!?"

Chris told me one of our other fraternity brothers was getting married, and everybody was staying at this hotel.

I wondered: *What are the odds that we're all staying at the exact same hotel in this tiny little beach town, at the same time?*

To put this in perspective, there are thousands of hotels in Florida, and dozens alone in St. Augustine Beach, yet they chose the exact one where I was holding a conference.

They asked, "What are you doing here? I know this is your company but had no idea you were hosting events."

I went on to explain what I was doing and how I invited my private clients down here to meet because it'd be a great spot to spend time together and get some work done.

"Holy cow, I didn't realize your business had grown so big," said Chris.

"Well, it's not like a typical business you're probably imagining," I said. "I mean, most of my clients are online. And every so often, we host in-person meetups. I decided that since I was going to be down here, I'd invite some people to join me."

"Well, how long are you down here for?" they asked.

"We're here for about six weeks," I said.

And as soon as I said that, their jaws just dropped. "Six weeks?!"

"Well, how long are you guys here for CJ's wedding?" I asked.

Chris said, "Well, I was able to get three days off."

My other friend, Mike, said, "Yeah, I got two days off."

Finally, my other frat brother, Josh, said, "Yeah, I'm here for three or four days."

Each answer I got was between two to four days. I wasn't sure what to say, so I just looked around and said, "Well, that's great."

But … I could tell they were all curious to know how we were able to spend so much time away from home.

Ah, Semi-Retirement

Back in 2010, when I was 23 years old, I was working as a sales engineer for a commercial HVAC manufacturer. We sold air distribution equipment to mechanical contractors and building owners throughout Buffalo, NY.

If you've never worked in the construction business, just know that it can be brutal. High stress. Lots of angry people. Tons of things can (and do) go wrong. As the saying goes: "Poop flows downhill," and the manufacturer's reps are at the bottom of the hill. Yum.

One particular company in my territory was rather large. They were the "big boys" in town, and they knew it. They got all of the big jobs. They ran their reps through the wringer, always beating them down on price and mistreating them.

I did everything in my power to make sure they were happy, but it was never good enough. Regularly, they'd call me up and curse me out. They'd scream and tell me how worthless and useless I was. They would call my boss and beg to have me fired. True story.

For almost four years, I endured their verbal lashings, because I was terrified to lose their business. I thought my sales would plummet for sure. I thought my boss would fire me.

Eventually, though, I let them go as a client. And as soon as I did, something incredible happened. Something I never thought would be possible ...

I made more money than ever before!

At first glance, it didn't make sense. But even though they were my largest client, I hardly made any profit from their jobs, and they took the most amount of my time to service.

There's something amazing that happens when you let go of things in your life ...

More space opens up for better things to flow in.

When I released that client, I instantly had stress relief. More focus. More mental clarity. And more time to pursue more profitable customers and projects. Since that day, I've experienced this phenomenon of letting go again and again.

When I was working my corporate job, in the corporate grind, I was not living my best life. I was under immense amounts of stress. I was unhealthy, I was overweight, and I was not sleeping well. I was actually even sleep-walking because of how much stress I was under.

I was ecstatic if I got more than two weeks of vacation per year. Sadly, that was the norm. But now, I'm taking six weeks off in a row and enjoying a fantastic lifestyle as a semi-retired professional.

If you were to ask me 10 years ago … heck, even just 5 years ago, if I'd be able to spend over a month, every single year, down at the beach, I'd have said you were crazy. I'd have thought that maaaaaybe when I'm 55 or 65 years old, I could retire and be a Florida snowbird because that's what most people do.

They work their entire lives and save up their money, buy a condo, and retire down south somewhere. Exactly what my parents did. They bought a place in Florida after my dad retired. But here I am, just a 31-year-old guy, who's able to spend more time down in the Sunshine State than any of my other family members.

Every spring, my family and I drive down from upstate New York to St. Augustine Beach to escape the brutally cold winters. That beach is now, by far, my favorite place on earth. We spend just over a month there, enjoying the beach and the ocean, and having fun in the sun.

The beach is where my heart is. I love looking out over the ocean while hearing waves crash up on the beach. I love playing with my kids in the sand. I love the heavy rains that come and cool down the humid air. Everything about the beach resonates with who I am as a person.

I have two very young kids, Dominic and Leah. At the time of this writing, Dominic is just about to turn four years old, and Leah is just about to turn one. I've been married to my beautiful wife Maryjo for almost nine years.

I never could have imagined back then that I'd be living my dream life by packaging and selling my intellectual property online.

Once I started to see what building an expert-based business allowed me to do by leveraging the power of both marketing and delivery online, I realized that we all have intellectual property we can leverage. Expertise that people want and will pay for.

By teaching others how to take advantage of this online model, anyone can live a dream lifestyle that's nothing short of extraordinary. We live in amazing times. It's absolutely the greatest gift I could have ever imagined.

If I could go back in time, this is the book I would have handed to my fraternity brothers when we ran into each other in that hotel in St. Augustine Beach, Florida. This is essentially how I went from working a high-stress, dead-end job to becoming semi-retired.

I'm handing it to **you**, now.

BONUS SECTION

BONUS #1: Create Your Identity Value Creation Avatar

It's time to make some lightbulbs go on in your mind. I want you to take action. Without action, no results are going to happen.

You're going to create your Identity Value Creation Avatar in 1–2 sentences. This is for internal use only, meaning your customers/audience will not see this. It's for your clarity and reference only.

Here's the framework:

- I help **(target market)** become **(a new identity)** through the use of **(my methodology, system, or process)**. What this means is: **(Explain your primary benefits here)**.

- Example: I help **course marketers** become **semi-retired** by becoming **High Ticket Course Experts.** What this means is: **They'll never have to struggle for clients again because they'll know how to instantly create demand in any market for their products and services.**

Ready to take action? This is the first step in clarifying your avatar and message. And to encourage you, I want to bribe you to do your homework.

Go to highticketcourses.com/bonuses and input your Identity Value Creation Avatar (IVC Avatar). Once you post it there, I've got a special gift that I will physically mail to you.

Bonus #2: Sales Scripts Swipe File

The Perfect Pitch

This is how you start collecting your testimonials if you don't have any. You say:

"Listen, this is my methodology. This is what I've done to get success, and I'm confident I can bring other people success as well. What I'd like is to work one-on-one with clients like you, because I'm planning on developing this as a course.

"Because I'm looking for my first clients, and because I'm going to be personally working with them as I validate and prove my methods, my one-on-one rates will be going up substantially higher once the course is published.

"But since this is the first stage of launching the program, I'm giving a drastically reduced rate for my direct, personal attention and fees. Plus, I'm guaranteeing success for anyone that I work with one-on-one.

"So, Mr. Prospect, if you're interested in the end result, I'm going to help you myself and personally guarantee that we get that outcome together because I'm looking to build my portfolio of case studies and testimonials.

"If you take action now and decide to reach your goals with me … First, you're going to have my full, undivided attention on a one-on-one basis at a drastically reduced rate. And second, I'm guaranteeing that you're going to achieve the result you want."

You position your problem as their benefit. You position your challenge of not having any testimonials as an advantage for your prospect.

That is how you get started. By selling something before it's ever created. Let them know how this gives them the highest probability of success with guaranteed results, or you'll continue to work with them until they have success.

Four-Step Conversation to Conversion (Validation and 3-Question Close)

Use the following script to qualify your leads that come through your mini webinar funnel *after* they submit an assessment form and *before* your enrollment call.

Doing this will transform your call with them from a "strategy session" to a Q&A call, and your sales conversions will drastically increase.

Validation

You should be able to figure this out once they submit their assessment form. Once you develop the right assessment form and the right questions, you should have a pretty clear idea —yes or no—if you can help them. If the answer is no, then you want to make sure that you let them know right away, so you don't waste your time on a call.

Sample Conversation: "I looked over your form, and I want to ask some follow-up questions. I have 100 percent confidence that assuming those questions come back as I think they will, there is no doubt in my mind that I can help you achieve (your end result)."

Question 1: Why Me?

In the 3-Question Close, the first question they need to answer is why they're coming to you instead of anyone else. Above all else, you need to make sure they're buying into your methodology.

Ask them the following questions:

- Have you taken the time to learn about my methodology?
- Have you taken the time to learn about my solution?
- Did you have an "Aha!" moment that my solution is unique?
- Does it make sense to you?

You want them to say, "Yes, I've watched your webinar, and I understand it."

Then, you want them to tell you why they like your method versus what they've been doing in the past. Ideally, they'll use your branded language. Listen for the terminologies that you've created as they explain to you why they're choosing you.

This is how you get them to essentially sell themselves.

Question 2: Now or Later?

The now-or-later question is the urgency question. It's a simple question where you ask them, "Hey, is this something that you're looking to make a decision on right now? Or is this a later-on decision?"

Sample Question: "If at the end of this call I feel that there's a definite way that I can help you, and if I provide value to your situation, are you looking to make a yes-or-no decision on this now, or are you just looking and you want to decide a couple of weeks from now?"

> **If later:** "Okay, perfect. If that's the case, that's totally cool. What I want you to do is to come back to me when you're ready to make a yes-or-no decision. That way, we can talk about the appropriate offer that's right for you. If we talk about it now, things could change. Availability can change between now and when you're ready to make that decision, and I don't want to give you the wrong information."
>
> **If now**: Move on to Question 3.

Question 3: Do You Have the Investment?

In the investment-range question, I tell them: Assuming that this is a good fit, the investment in our services ranges from X to Y.

Sample Question: "Our levels of investment start at $2,000 and go all the way up to $15,000. Does that fit your budget? Do you have the budget available now to reach your goals?"

> **If the answer is no**: "Okay, that's totally fine. Listen, we may offer some lower-level programs in the future, so I would love for you to stay tuned, but at this point, it doesn't make sense for us to continue the conversation. So let's just part ways, and I'll send you some additional great content down the road."
>
> **If the answer is yes**: "Perfect. Let's continue this conversation, and I'll see you on the call to discuss more."

Sunday, Jun 30

Hey   - it's Joel Erway from The Webinar Agency. Just saw   JE
your assessment form come through. Wanted to text you with a
few followup questions based on what I saw with your
assessment form to work out if or how I can help you. If I feel like I
can help you we'll schedule a call to discuss further. That cool
with you?

6:14 AM

Sounds good, Joel. Send em my way.

12:45 PM

Sweet. You get a chance to watch the mini webinar   JE

1:08 PM

Watched a few videos last night, but don't believe I watched the
mini webinar. Shoot me a link and I'll watch it this morning.

1:23 PM

Https://Newwaytolaunch.com

1:24 PM

Thanks. Really like what I watched so far. Walking into a class
now, I'll get back to you after I watch the rest.

1:38 PM

Just finished watching it. Im interested.

2:55 PM

Cool. What about our methodology in that mini webinar makes
you think this is the right methodology for your launch?

3:12 PM

More than the methodology, I'm buying your expertise. That said,
I like the simplicity, short timeframe to validate, and scalability.

I believe the investment, pain, and desires of my target audience
are big enough to drive them to buy the premium product; not
only that, but they have proven to be quick decision makers /
impulse buyers.

3:55 PM

BM Oh, and I love that you guys do all the work for me, allowing me
to focus on serving my customers.
3:57 PM

I think there's something there for sure. The time share market is   JE
in a lot of pain.

I always prefer to be upfront and transparent about our services
so we don't waste your time if it's not a fit.

Our minimum engagement for strategy starts at $5k. And
minimum engagement for implementation starts at $30k.

Obviously we will want to hop on the phone before we commit to
anything.

Does your budget allow for that level of investment to reach your
goals for this project.
4:56 PM

BM My budget allows for it.
5:02 PM

Awesome. Let's grab a spot here at your convenience   JE
meetme.so/joelanway
5:36 PM

BONUS #3: Build Your Client-Warmup Machine

The client-warmup machine is your strategic use of content marketing. If you follow me for any length of time, you will probably see that I pump out a ton of content. I have a team member who takes my content, repurposes it, and shares it.

When done correctly, this acts as an accelerator for nurturing your audience. When done incorrectly, it's a complete waste of time. I will tell you again: If you are not in Phase 2 of the trajectory, you do not need to be focusing on content marketing at all.

Here are some rules that you should follow for accelerated results with content marketing done the right way:

- They should already be in your sphere of influence (not traffic-type content, SEO, etc.)
- You should be creating content that both repels and attracts. Repel the potential clients you don't want while attracting the clients you do want. (Don't worry about repelling people. If you repel people, you're going to attract and build a closer bond to the ones who were really most attracted to your message.)

Types of Content

There are eight types of content that I focus on that have been the biggest needle-movers in my business:

- Lifestyle (i.e. my 4x4 week)
- Memes
- Authoritative (look who's talking about me, where I've been featured)
- Process/Methodology
- Mechanisms
- Pain/Problem
- Solution/Value
- Testimonials

These types of content can be cycled through over and over again in a repetitive fashion. That gets results, causing people to follow you because they want to learn more about what you do.

Ask yourself:

- What stories make me look good? Where have I been featured, etc.?
- How can I talk about my process/methodology in a way that relates to my audience?
- How can I take different angles about each piece of content so it relates to a different segment of my audience?
- Do I have any unique mechanisms for how I deliver my process?

This is what's going to warm up those people who have raised their hand, who are interested, but who are not yet ready to buy.

Audience & Channels

The most valuable asset that you can acquire is an audience. They will keep you afloat when times are tough.

Be smart about acquiring an audience and maintaining momentum. Expanding into other channels and platforms gives you stability and greater reach because, believe it or not, there is a segment of every audience that will not respond to ads. And that's okay because they will listen to podcasts, or they will read social media, or they will check you out if you are mentioned by somebody else. Don't get too narrow-minded with your audience outreach.

When you're first starting out, yes, you only focus on one channel, one platform, one offer, and one minimum viable funnel—because that's all you need to get to $30K per month. But maintaining that stability will require you to branch out.

So what are the types of channels that really move the needle?

- Ads—Google Search, YouTube, Facebook, LinkedIn
- Email—extremely powerful asset that you own
- Groups—your own and others
- Social—Instagram, Facebook, LinkedIn, YouTube
- Podcast—your own and others

Ads

If you don't own an audience first, this is where you can start. This is what I use to amplify what's working for my content marketing. Ads are the single greatest growth tool and time-saver in your arsenal, and they're still relatively cheap for what you get in return.

You can make a killing off of ads if you have a High Ticket program. It's still relatively cheap for what you get in return because you're building your audience, your assets, your offers, and your revenue.

Email

Do not sleep on this, regardless of what you hear about open rates. The ability to market and communicate directly to a list that you own is invaluable. This effort alone will support you for as long as you are in this market. This is great for internal promotions, which is also known as free money. You can have a one-to-one relationship with your audience through email. It's extremely powerful and excellent for leadership.

Groups

When you get people to join a group and that group grows, it doesn't matter how big it is. People are going to say, "Wow, look at that group!" and they're going to follow you. It's great for maintaining engagement and building a bond around a common idea. It's not so great at getting everyone to see your message; regardless, it's still an excellent social-proof leadership tool.

Social

Facebook, Twitter, YouTube, Instagram, LinkedIn, and all of the ever-increasing number of social media platforms all have their pros and cons. This is dependent on where you and your customers spend their time. You can be active on one platform and repurpose your content for other platforms. There are several social media scheduling and tracking tools to make cross-posting easier and more effective. Do an online search for "Social Media Posting and Scheduling Tools" to find the right scheduler for you.

Podcasts

This is my sleeper pick and easily my absolute favorite. It has given me the highest ROI plus enjoyment factor. It can be a great way to create pillar content and use that to be repurposed into other forms of content. People can listen to podcasts when they're traveling anywhere—on the airplane, on walks, and in the car. Being in their ear is extremely powerful, and it's extremely easy to produce.

Your Invisible Safety Net

The key takeaway here is that content is your invisible safety net once you start building your audience (Phases 2-3). Start out by creating content for your audience—even as little as just one time per week—as you're building your email list. Give them a new insight, a new "aha" moment, and invite them to book a call. That's all you need to do to start this process.

As you progress, hire a team member to do this for you. There are tons of talented content marketers out there who love creating content and would be excited to do this on your behalf. This will be one of the best team investments that you can make in your business.

Ask yourself:

- What do I enjoy doing? Is it podcasting? Is it writing? Is it filming videos? (Whatever your answer is, that is what you should focus on.)
- How can I create one simple email every week to my audience?
- What are the top 10–20 podcast shows in my audience that would be interested in hearing my story?

This is your client-warmup machine, your invisible safety net.

ACKNOWLEDGMENTS

To Maryjo:

There's a reason I don't teach my network to write books as a method to get clients. Because to produce a great one, it's really friggin' hard :) None of this would have been possible without my wife, Maryjo, and her push to get this to the finish line. My ADD brain wanted to throw in the towel on more than one (or twelve) occasions.

To Dominic and Leah:

Knowledge is power. There's not much in this world that we can control. But one thing that will shape your world more than anything is the information and content that you not only consume but also create. Everything you can possibly want to learn is at your fingertips. Take charge and take ownership of your lives by maintaining a constant appetite for learning.

To my editorial team, Lori, Kathy, and Katie:

What started out in my mind as a 30-day project turned into a 12-month+ project that transformed into two complete rewrites, multiple title revisions, avatar adjustments, and much more. Most editorial teams probably would have quit on me. But I am eternally grateful that I discovered you to help take what's inside this jumbled mess of a brain and brilliantly distill it into what you're reading right now. Thank you!

To my current clients and customers:

Thank you for giving me the platform and opportunity to be able to use this book to turn hundreds of happy clients into potentially thousands. It's the hundreds of hours that I've spent with you that helped me shape the core content of this book that will impact far more people than I could have ever imagined.

ABOUT THE AUTHOR

Joel Erway is the founder of The Webinar Agency and the creator of the High Ticket Courses (HTC) Model. His methods have generated over $50 million collectively for his clients, his students, and his own businesses.

He is a contributor to Entrepreneur.com and has been interviewed on dozens of podcasts, including *The Mike Dillard Show*, Roland Frasier's *Business Lunch* podcast, and more. He is also the host of two different podcasts: *Sold With Webinars* and *Experts Unleashed*.

He lives with his wife and two children in Lewiston, NY.

To find out more about Joel Erway, check out JoelErway.com.